AMERICAN SIGN LANGUAGE

Lexical and Grammatical Notes
With Translation Exercises

LEXICAL AND
GRAMMATICAL NOTES
WITH TRANSLATION EXERCISES

American
Sign Language

Harry W. Hoemann
Psychology Department
Bowling Green
State University

Foreword by
Dennis Cokely

Introduction by
Terrence J. O'Rourke

Illustrated by
Shirley A. Hoemann

National Association of the Deaf
814 Thayer Ave.
Silver Spring, Md. 20910

AMERICAN SIGN LANGUAGE

Lexical and Grammatical Notes with Translation Exercises
by Harry W. Hoemann

Library of Congress Catalogue Number 75-34954
Printed in the United States of America
Second Printing January 1982
Third Printing November 1983

Table of Contents

Foreword

In recent years, there has been a tremendous increase in the number of sign classes offered throughout the country. More and more colleges and universities are now accepting Sign Language for credit and in partial fulfillment of language requirements. Courses in Sign Language are now being offered in high schools and elementary schools. It is truly exciting and encouraging to see such interest in manual communication. However, with regard to the field of Sign Language learning and instruction, there are some critical issues that warrant discussion and several principles that require consideration.

Perhaps the most crucial issue facing the field of Sign Language learning and teaching is not how, but rather, what. Too often students and teachers are uncertain as to what their object of study is or should be. A basic starting point must be this: American Sign Language is not English. American Sign Language (also referred to as A.S.L., Ameslan, or simply Sign) has its own morphology and syntax which is distinct from English. While it is possible to utilize the lexicon of A.S.L. and the syntax of English to communicate manually, this is not to be considered American Sign Language. Consider the Frenchman who uses the lexicon of English and the syntax of French to utter, "I myself call myself John." This double reflexive, which is required by French syntax, would be considered an extremely peculiar variety of English at best, and more than likely ungrammatical.

The point is, of course, that A.S.L. is a language distinct from English. It is not enough to teach or learn the lexicon of A.S.L., utilize English syntax, and then claim to be a student of A.S.L. An example may help to further illustrate this point:

English: Have you been to California?
A.S.L.: Finish touch California?

Now, of course, it is entirely possible to sign the first sentence using A.S.L. vocabulary. However, the missing element, A.S.L. syntax, is what distinguishes A.S.L. from a mere manual coding of English.

A second critical issue that bears discussion is the nature of language learning and language teaching. It is a sad fact (perhaps owing to the relative recent interest in A.S.L.) that, while there have been considerable advances in the theory and methodology of language learning, there has been little application of these advances to the field of Sign Language instruction. The simple fact is that the vast majority of sign language classes are nothing more than vocabulary lessons. In part, this failure is due to the limited instructional materials available to teachers. Until recently, the only materials available consisted of nothing more than sign lists (the term dictionaries is inappropriate, since these lists provide neither etymology nor co-occurrence restrictions). While recent materials have attempted to avoid such a simple listing, they do not provide ample contextual examples of A.S.L. usage to permit the student to induce the syntactic rules needed to acquire competency in the language. It is worth noting that in no other language learning situation (except possibly for the "dead" languages) is a student given a word list for memorization and then required to speak the language. And yet, this seems to be the main thrust of a great many sign classes.

At this point, it may be worthwhile to examine a few key principles upon which a successful course in A.S.L. should be based. While these are by no means the only factors to be considered in teaching A.S.L., they warrant careful consideration in the successful learning and teaching of American Sign Language.

I. *There should be a period of readiness and preparation for learning the language.* This is especially critical, because the learner is suddenly required to utilize an unfamiliar sensory channel for communication—the eyes, not the ears. Since A.S.L. is a spatial language in motion, the student must now become accustomed to encoding and decoding meaning from such factors as movement, position, hand shape, and facial expression. Exercises in visual discrimination and visual memory should not be considered too far-fetched in assisting students in acquiring facility with the visual channel. Expressively, the learner also needs to gain facility with the various hand shapes, movements, and positions needed for the production of signs. This readiness level should be analogous to the initial stages of learning a spoken language —various pronunciation and listening exercises, which aim to impart expressive and receptive familiarity with the phonetic system of the language.

II. *Development of receptive skills in A.S.L. should precede expressive skills.* While this statement may seem obvious upon first reading, it bears closer examination. Although this principle of "receptive before expressive" is employed in almost all foreign language learning classes and is, in fact, the procedure followed by infants in language acquisition, it is rarely, if ever, implemented in the instruction of Sign Language. On the contrary, most sign classes devote much time and energy teaching students "how to" sign, but very little in "how to read" signs. To overcome this failure, instructors must be convinced of the fact that development of receptive skills fosters a predisposition in the student, which results in the development of expressive skills. Such an approach has serious implications for the instructor in the areas of materials selection, class format and technique. It means that, insofar as possible, the teacher must assume the role of language model for the class; it also means that the teacher must be prepared to utilize appropriate methods of contrastive analysis to assist in the learning process; finally, it means that the teacher must select those materials which provide the students with satisfactory models of A.S.L.

III. *Fingerspelling should be taught relatively late in an A.S.L. course.* Currently, in most classes, fingerspelling is taught in the first or second class. The rationale for this is that "it is easy to learn, provides the students with initial success and enables them to communicate with the deaf quickly." While some of these points are valid, nonetheless the long range implications merit consideration. First, while it is true that the manual alphabet utilizes the majority of hand shapes needed for signing, these hand shapes should be taught without attaching any alphabetic value to them. The hand shapes are important; however, it may be simply a coincidence that they also function as manual representations of English orthography. Second, the role of fingerspelling in A.S.L. must not be overestimated. It may be successfully argued that such lexical units as C-A-R, J-O-B and B-A-L-L can be considered signs because of the ease, frequency and speed of execution. Third, by allowing the student to gain facility with the manual alphabet early in the course, the teacher runs the risk of diminishing the students' motivation to acquire lexical items later in the course.

The student is less likely to work at building a vocabulary bank if he feels he can always rely upon fingerspelling. The point under discussion here is simply that while the manual alphabet has provided a convenient vehicle for teaching the hand shapes of A.S.L., its inclusion in an A.S.L. course or its place in the course must be seriously considered.

IV. *There should be a deaf informant in every A.S.L. course.* The optimal situation, of course, is when the instructor is a native user of A.S.L. and can serve as both instructor and informant. While hearing loss is not a necessary correlate to native competency in A.S.L., it must be stated that by far the vast majority of native users are deaf. Consequently, it would seem that the ideal situation in an A.S.L. course is when the instructor is deaf. All too often, however, the instructor is a hearing person who possesses less than native competence in A.S.L. This situation may occur in colleges, for example, where there are other criteria for teaching than competency in the Language. Since there are limited materials available which effectively deal with A.S.L., any hearing person teaching a course in A.S.L. should seriously consider the use of a deaf informant in a team teaching situation. Even if the instructor is a native user of A.S.L., the value of other native users cannot be discounted. This will be further discussed in the next section. For the moment, consider the advantages of a deaf instructor or a deaf informant. Paragraphs and stories can be elicited which provide actual samples of A.S.L. usage; contrastive features of A.S.L. and English can be illustrated; translation exercises can be undertaken; questions and discussions about deafness itself can be dealt with. If the instructor is fortunate enough to find enough willing informants, there is nothing better than to provide one-to-one interaction. The deaf informant can also be invaluable in assisting the instructor in evaluating students' facility with A.S.L. Until the day when there are ample video-tapes and films of A.S.L. usage, there is no better way of providing students with idiomatic, contextual A.S.L. usage than through a native user.

V. *Students should be exposed to as wide a variety of signers as possible.* Students have often been frustrated by the experience of being able to decode the signs of their teacher but being unable to decode the signing of deaf individuals they encounter. Because A.S.L. varies more from user to user (because of physiology, facial subtleties, use of positioning and other factors) than spoken languages tend to do, it is imperative that the students learn to accept, recognize and deal with these differences. For this reason, it is highly desirable that as wide a range of models be provided as possible. Consider some of the following characteristics which contribute to an individual signer's style: Dominance (left- or right-handedness), beards or moustaches, maximum or minimum lip movement, sex, etc. Any one of these factors could conceivably prove to be an obstacle to decoding a signed message. Thus, the teacher should attempt to provide sufficient models for the student to become comfortable in dealing with these differences.

VI. *Care should be exercised in the selection of materials for a course in A.S.L.* It should be obvious from the above discussions that the teacher should avoid a vocabulary-oriented approach in teaching A.S.L. Currently, however, the vast majority of materials available on the market consist of mere word lists, and their value in imparting competence in A.S.L. must be suspect. While these materials do fulfill a useful function as reference tools, they fail to provide any syntactic information about A.S.L. Since A.S.L. is a spatial language in motion, undoubtedly the best materials are video-tapes and films. If the teacher has access to tape or film equipment, it may be possible to produce materials geared to class pace and need. However, in preparation of such materials, caution should be exercised so as to provide an ample variety of contexts for study. Language learning principles hold that vocabulary should be learned in context and not in isolation. Thus, a film or tape which merely demonstrates lexical items is of extremely limited value as an instructional tool—a reference tool possibly, but certainly not a vehicle for learning. In selection of materials, the teacher should be guided by the following rule of thumb: Vocabulary and syntax in context.

It is hoped that this discussion of principles and factors involved in the teaching and learning of American Sign Language has provided the reader with the mindset or frame of reference needed to take full advantage of this book of Sign Language translations. Students and teachers of A.S.L. should truly be indebted to the author for providing this corpus of translations. Apart from the actual texts, the grammatical notes are invaluable aids in attaining a working knowledge of certain lexical and syntactic features of A.S.L. With the publication of this book, students and teachers now have access to realistic samples of A.S.L. which, if studied carefully, should lead to a greater theoretical and practical understanding of the language. It is also hoped that this book merely marks the beginning of a new era of materials available in the teaching and learning of A.S.L. Someday, hopefully in the not too distant future, this book will be but one of many of its kind; someday, teachers and students will have a large quantity of films and video-tapes available for their use; someday, American Sign Language will, unequivocably, be accorded the status it deserves. This book represents a major step in those directions.

Dennis Cokely
September 30, 1975.

Author's Preface

This book is dedicated to the hundreds of deaf persons who, during the past twenty years, have graciously shared with me their day to day interests, their philosophical passions, and their deeply human concerns via a communicative channel that I have come to respect as a unique and powerful system. This book was written to call attention to some of the salient features of that system.

It is tempting to review here the history of the American Sign Language and to deplore the stigma that has, from time to time, been attached to it by well-intentioned professionals. But I prefer to take an optimistic view. The study of history, as one of my colleagues at Bowling Green once remarked, is the study of people's mistakes. The future is laid out before us as an opportunity to correct them. It is enough to know history so as not to repeat it. One need not recite it.

For the past five years I have taught the American Sign Language to undergraduate students at Bowling Green State University. They, too, deserve a large measure of credit for the preparation of this text, since the course was originally offered in response to student requests. Moreover, their desire to learn to communicate with deaf persons clearly required a commitment from their instructor to do more than merely show them how to execute a few hundred signs. There is no challenge more intellectually stimulating than a group of enthusiastic students. I cherish my association with them.

The Bowling Green State University academic community is also deserving of mention. The Psychology Department has provided a setting in which the American Sign Language can be taught in the context of the psychological implications of deafness. The Departments of Speech and Special Education have supported the course with student enrollment and with faculty consultation. The Undergraduate Committee of the Psychology Department and the Academic Council of the College of Arts and Sciences reviewed the prospectus for the course and approved it for four hours of undergraduate credit, listing it as Psychology 324, American Sign Language of the Deaf, in the University publication of Course Descriptions. The Graduate College and the College of Arts and Sciences have enabled graduate students in Psychology, Speech, and Rehabilitation to participate as advanced students engaged in independent study. The Faculty Development Program Implementation Committee has provided funds for instructional materials.

The preparation of this publication was aided by the J. Preston Levis Regional Computer Center, whose IBM 360/75 computer stored the text during the preparation of the manuscript. Access to the computer was provided through the LAPLUME Text Processing System developed by Charles M. Bernstein, Department of Computational Services, Bowling Green State University.

Of particular interest to the users of this manual is the contribution of Patrick T. Fitzgerald and the staff of WBGU-TV, who produced broadcast-quality color videotapes of the American Sign Language versions of the paragraphs in this volume. It is our expectation that a copy of this videotape will be made available at minimal cost to instructors in Sign Language classes who are using this manual. Information regarding the accompanying videotapes may be obtained by writing the author, Dr. Harry W. Hoemann, Psychology Department, Bowling Green State University, Bowling Green, OH 43403.

The contents of this manual have also been enriched by understandings of Sign Language and its use that have emerged from the conduct of research supported by National Institutes of Health Research Grant NS-09590, "The Development of Communication Skills in Deaf and Hearing Children," from the National Institute of Neurological Diseases and Stroke. Although the research reports generated by this project are published elsewhere, my role as project director and principal investigator for the project provided many opportunities to observe the communicative behavior of deaf children, to consult with specialists in deafness and Sign Language studies, and to review the growing body of literature dealing with Sign Languages. A list of recommended readings has been included in this volume to guide interested readers to some of the literature that has informed the research that I have conducted.

I should also like to mention the National Association of the Deaf for playing a role in the development of these materials that has gone beyond merely serving as publisher. The possibility that this manual might be of value to the Communicative Skills Program, directed by T. J. O'Rourke, provided a major incentive from the beginning to undertake the project. Moreover, the mutual trust that has characterized our collaboration with the National Association of the Deaf in other projects, the *Sign Language Flash Cards* and the *Children's Sign Language Playing Cards,* has made this venture a particularly satisfying experience.

The vocabulary lists associated with each lesson are keyed to two National Association of the Deaf publications, the *Sign Language Flash Cards* and *A Basic Course in Manual Communication*. Such presentations of the citation forms of signs from the American Sign Language are clearly a necessary aid in the mastery of a functional vocabulary. It is expected that one or both of these sources will be used in conjunction with this manual.

The justification for an additional text rests with the conviction that the American Sign Language is best learned through translations of meaningful prose. When American Sign Language messages are embedded in a meaningful context, the citation forms of the signs are modified so as to fit that context. Modulations appear which are not listed in publications of a Sign Language vocabulary. The citation forms of signs are rarely seen in real-life settings. One reason students of American Sign Language are often frustrated as they try to understand deaf people conversing in signs is that the students are looking for the citation forms of signs that they have learned from a vocabulary listing, and all they see are modulated signs and modifications of citation forms required by the situation or context. Moreoever, knowing American Sign Language requires much more than knowing a few hundred signs for English cognates. It requires mastery of the many strategies used by deaf people to communicate effectively. Some of these strategies can only be observed in longer passages of American Sign Language texts. The translation exercises presented here are designed to provide examples of the unique and powerful strategies that may be used by deaf people to encode a meaning that has been specified in an English original.

These acknowledgments could name many more names. I trust that the many individuals who have made specific contributions either to my knowledge of American Sign Language or to the preparation of this volume will accept this general statement of gratitude as a sincere attempt to add a personal touch. I thank you individually and collectively for your help and encouragement.

Finally, I would like to pay special tribute to Shirley A. Hoemann, my wife, both for the specific contribution that she has made to this volume by creating its illustrations and for her general support and encouragement during all stages of its preparation. Having her as a colleague in this project has been especially gratifying.

Harry W. Hoemann
September, 1975

Introduction

The first known dictionary of signs used by the American deaf was printed in Baton Rouge, Louisiana at the *Morning Comet* office in 1856. This 50-page book by James S. Brown was entitled *A Vocabulary of Mute Signs*. It was not, however, until 1910 when J. Schuyler Long published *The Sign Language: A Manual of Signs* that a fairly definitive and popular dictionary of signs became available. Although a number of other dictionaries were published by educators of the deaf and religious workers with the deaf during the next fifty years, (1910-1960), only one other dictionary received widespread and popular use—Daniel D. Higgins', *How to Talk to the Deaf* published by the author in St. Louis in 1923.

The decade from 1960-1970 saw a tremendous increase in the publication of not only sign language dictionaries, but also formal linguistic research on signs as used by deaf people in America. William C. Stokoe, Jr's 1960 monograph *Sign Language Structure: An Outline of the Visual Communication Systems of the American Deaf* published by the University of Buffalo was the cornerstone of linguistic description of what was termed American Sign Language (later called "Ameslan" by Louie J. Fant, Jr.). Stokoe's later (1965) *A Dictionary of American Sign Language on Linguistic Principles* which was prepared along with Dorothy C. Casterline and Carl G. Croneberg is still the most definitive work on American Sign Language yet produced although its use has been more or less limited to academic and research areas.

The publication in 1961 of C. J. Springer's *Talking with the Deaf*, an updated version of Daniel D. Higgins *How to Talk to the Deaf*, and the 1963 publication of David O. Watson's *Talk with Your Hands* and Lottie Riekehof's *Talk to the Deaf* provided the first dictionaries in over forty years. However, it was Louie J. Fant, Jr. who in 1964 published *Say It with Hands* who provided the first departure from the dictionary format for presenting signs. Fant's text, developed as part of a federal (Vocational Rehabilitation Administration) grant to the District of Columbia Association of the Deaf which later became the national Communicative Skills Program, was the first to provide practice material for learning signs as a language and thus the first to go beyond the vocabulary or dictionary approach to learning signs. Willard Madsen's *Conversational Sign Language II: An Intermediate-Advanced Manual* was also developed under this VRA grant program. However it was not published until 1972.

With the publication in 1970 of *A Basic Course in Manual Communication* by the NAD's Communicative Skills Program, a new era began. The revised 1973 edition of *ABC* as it has become known, along with accompanying teaching and learning aids including George Propp's *Sign by Design* and the "See 'N' Sign" viewers, has become the singularly most popular and used text on the market with sales of over 1000 copies a week. The text, however, does not provide exercises for the acquisition of a grammatical understanding of American Sign Language. This is left up to the instructor.

Louie J. Fant, Jr.'s 1972 publication of *Ameslan: An Introduction to American Sign Language* provided another milestone in the development of sign language instructional materials. For the first time, a text that went beyond the lexical elements of American Sign Language was provided. The basic rules of Ameslan are presented and contrasted, at times, with those of English. The signs and their combinations are taught through the use of poetry, conversation, dialogues and monologues. Film packages that cover each of the 14 lessons in the text are also available. This text was thus the first attempt to teach ASL as a language. Linguistic research which had been generated by the work of Stokoe had left little doubt that the American Sign Language used by deaf persons was a unique and fully-developed language system as complex as any in the world. It was for Fant to attempt to provide a means for teaching this language in its pure sense.

The early 1970's also saw the development of another phenomenon regarding the teaching of signs. A number of groups and individuals attempted to expand the lexicon of American signs and to develop an arbitrary set of symbols to represent English functional morphemes in signs. These people, mostly educators of the deaf, thus developed a number of different ways to try to represent English in signs. The most notable of these books is *Signing Exact English* by Gerilee Gustason, Donna Pfetzing, and Ester Zawolkow (1972).

Now, for the first time, a text which fully capitalizes on the teaching of and research on signs which has been done over the past 15 years is available to teachers and students of American Sign Language along with T.V. cassettes and soon-to-be developed Super-8 cartridge films. This book represents another milestone in the ever-present goal of the NAD to provide more and better materials for instruction in the language of signs. Dr. Hoemann is to be commended for his latest contribution to the field.

Terrence J. O'Rourke, Director
NAD Communicative Skills Program

Lesson One

ENGLISH ORIGINAL

Rain

A little while ago I thought the rain might stop, but now it is raining harder than ever. The wind has changed. Now it is coming from the north, and the temperature is dropping. If it gets much colder, it will turn to snow. I want the rain to go away. It has been raining every day lately, and it is really monotonous. I have been bored stiff. What I want is some blue skies and some warm sunshine. I know we need rain for the sake of the farmers' crops. If there were no rain, everything would dry up and the crops would wither. I have an idea! Why doesn't it rain during the night and stop each morning? Or why doesn't it rain on Fridays and clear up on Saturdays? If I were in charge of the weather, I would see to it that Saturday and Sunday would always be pleasant. On Mondays, who cares? Let it rain.

SIGN LANGUAGE GLOSS

Rain

A-little-while-ago think me rain maybe stop. Now worse. Wind change (pause) now blow from north, and temperature drop. Happen temperature plunge (pause) will begin snow. Me want rain disappear. Every-day rain, rain, rain (pause) truly same, same, same. Me bored. Wish sky blue sunshine warm. True, know rain need for farmer their grow area. Rain disappear, all dry (pause) all wither. Idea! All-night rain, morning stop. Why not? Fridays rain, Saturdays nice. Why not? Me rule, make fine. Me decide Saturday Sunday always pleasant. Mondays (pause) Phooey! Let rain.

1

GRAMMATICAL NOTES ──────────────

A-little-while-ago The little finger side of the right fist is placed against or near the right cheek with the index finger extended. The index finger is wiggled backward several times. If it is a very short time ago that is intended, the head may be tilted slightly and the eyes squinted shut. If the thumb of the right hand is placed against or near the right cheek with the index finger extended, and the index finger is moved forward with a twist of the wrist, the sign means *later, after while.* Thus, a movement backward along the cheek refers to the past, *while ago, previously,* while a movement forward along the cheek refers to the future. Both signs may also be executed against the left palm. The left palm is held facing the right with the fingers pointing upward. An imaginary time line runs down the middle of the palm, so that movements forward refer to the future, while movements backward refer to the past.

think me A number of signs denoting mental activity are signed on the forehead. For *think,* the right index finger may be tapped to the forehead several times or trace small circles on the forehead. If the fingertips of the right hand are touched to the forehead, the sign means *know.* If the fist is knocked against the forehead, the sign means *stupid.* The back of the horizontal right "V" hand placed against the forehead means *ignorant.* The right "X" hand, fingertip pointing downward, moved downward in front of the forehead several times means *wise,* possibly referring to the depths of an intelligent mind. If the right hand wipes across the surface of the forehead, the sign means *forget.*

rain The "CLAW" hands (bent "5" hands) are traced downward several times in front of the face, imitating the streams of raindrops falling from the sky.

maybe Both hands are held, palm up, in front of the body, and the hands are raised and lowered alternately as if weighing something in the hands. The action is continued for a brief duration, and the facial expression and body posture imply indecision. This basic gesture is probably the origin of other signs which are executed similarly: *judge,* with the "F" hands, *which,* with thumbs-up "A" hands, *doubt,* with palms-down "S" hands. All of these signs are executed in the same location and with the same movement. They are differentiated from each other by the hand configuration and by the associated facial expression and body posture. The role of the hand configuration as a distinctive feature in signs such as these supports a conceptualization of American Sign Language as comprised of a finite set of structural features which may be combined in various ways to form its lexicon. The first formal presentation of such a model of Sign Language structure was made by William C. Stokoe, Jr., in 1960. This model has since been used as the basis for a dictionary of American Sign Language based on linguistic principles. Recent reformulations have extended the scope and utility of Stokoe's model of American Sign Langage structure. For additional information, consult the list of recommended readings at the close of this volume.

stop The general sign for *stop* brings the little-finger edge of the right palm down to a forceful stop against the upturned left palm. The sign refers primarily to something that is moving and that comes to a stop. But it can also be used for *stop* in other contexts as well. As an alternative, the sign for *rain* can be signed increasingly slowly until finally all downward movement ceases, implying that the downpour has subsided.

Now Both hands, palms-up, are brought down to a forceful stop at about waist level in front of the body.

worse The "V" hands, palms up, are held in front of the body, and they are brought together so that the wrists cross in a single swift movement. This sign is not as restricted in meaning as is the English word, *worse.* Usually it is taken in a negative sense, as in the present context. Under some circumstances, however, it can take on a positive tone. As an example, at a track meet at Gallaudet College, after one broad jumper jumped 18 feet, a by-stander pointed to another of the contestants and signed *He worse, 20.* Thus, the sign may actually imply anything excessive, which is usually bad but not necessarily so. The sign, *worse,* may be related to the sign for *multiply,* which is executed similarly, but with repeated movements instead of one decisive gesture.

Wind The hands are held, palms facing, in front of the body, and they are moved back and forth as if to set up a breeze.

change This sign is related to the sign for *become.* In both signs the hands exchange places, right for left, as they are turned over in front of the body. *Become* is signed with open hands, palm to palm. *Change* is signed with "A" or "X" hands. Ordinarily the right hand is placed below the left and is on top of the left in its final position, but the reverse is permissible. Left handed signing is observed quite frequently among Sign Language users. For this reason, almost any sign can be signed left handed and still be readily understood.

FIG. 1. *The aversive north wind is indicated by means of a natural gesture and appropriate facial expression.*

blow Ordinarily the same sign is used for *wind* and *blow.* However, in this case a natural gesture is more likely to be used. One possibility is for the hands to fan the face from an angle, as if throwing wind against it. The face should be turned aside with a dour expression to imply that the effect of the wind against the face is aversive (see Fig. 1).

from Like many signs referring to spatial relations, the left hand provides a point of reference, and the meaning of the sign is derived from the movement or position of the right hand relative to the left. In this case, the left index finger is extended, and the right "X" hand is brought toward the body from an initial position in which the curved right index finger is near or touching the left index finger. The right wrist may be twisted as the right hand is brought toward the body so that the right index finger makes an arc toward the chest. Since the right hand moves away *from* the left, the sign means *from.* In the present context, it is not absolutely necessary that the preposition be included, since the context would not support the notion that the wind is blowing toward the north.

north This is an initialized sign. The right "N" hand is moved in a direction that implies a northerly direction. By convention, this may be up, as on a map, or it may conform to true north by the compass relative to the position of the signer. But the usage is not as strict as that. A northerly direction may be adopted arbitrarily for the purposes of the immediate reference, much as a stage may have a window that is supposed to have a northern exposure regardless of how the stage and auditorium are actually situated with regard to the points of the compass. Once *north* has been indicated relative to the signer, if the other points of the compass are referenced, their directions should be consistent with the first one, but this is not absolutely necessary. The other points of the compass are indicated by means of the other initials: "E" for *east,* "S" for *south,* and "W" for *west.* The same kind of gesture symbol is used to indicate *right* (the right "R" hand moved off to the signer's right) and *left* (the right

3

or left "L" hand moved off to the signer's left).

and This is the coordinate conjunction, and it serves the same function as in English, to join two similar constructions. The right "5" hand is held with the palm facing left in front of the body. As it is moved toward the right, the fingers are clustered together. The sign implies taking what is already a matter of record, localized at the left, and bringing it across to the right where it can be linked up to what is about to follow. The sign is often omitted, since a pause can often carry the same meaning. The hand configuration of the right hand in the final position of the sign for *and,* with the fingertips touching as the fingers are clustered together, is what is meant by the "AND" hand elsewhere in this volume.

temperature The sign for *temperature* represents the column of mercury in a thermometer. In one version, the right index finger moves up and down in small movements against the left palm, which faces outward. If the signer has any doubt as to whether the receiver will understand this sign for *temperature,* he may execute the sign with an inquiring expression on his face, perhaps even signing, *You know?* and await confirmation that the receiver has understood before he goes on to sign *drop.*

drop If this sign is executed too quickly, the receiver may infer that the temperature has already dropped. One way to distinguish between the present progressive tense and the past tense in American Sign Language is to execute the sign for the verb slowly or repeatedly so as to imply that the action is going on now. Of course, to remove all doubt, the signer may sign *now* before the verb. If *now* had not already been used in this sentence, that would be a reasonable strategy. Since it has been used, as an alternative, the index finger may be brought down relatively slowly on the left palm to imply that the temperature is falling slowly but steadily. The amount of the fall can be indicated by using the left palm as a frame of reference, and the farther down the left palm the finger goes, the more the temperature is said to be falling.

Happen Both hands are held, palms up, index fingers extended, in front of the body. They are turned over so that in the final position the palms are down. This sign is frequently used to express what is stated in English as *It happened that.* In this case, the context implies a condition, *If it happens that.* The same sign is sometimes used to introduce a story in much the same way that stories in English begin, *Once upon a time it happened that.* In English this usage is somewhat stilted and is relatively confined to story telling, especially fairy tales. In American Sign Language, however, the sign, *happen,* is used very frequently to signal that it is an event that is the subject of the discourse. The subsequent signs then present information about the event.

temperature plunge Although there is no conventional sign listed in the published dictionaries for *plunge* as distinct from *fall* in connection with the temperature, a simple distortion of the existing sign can convey exactly this nuance. The index finger can be inverted so as to point downward, and the signer can drive it vigorously downward along the left palm (see Fig. 2).

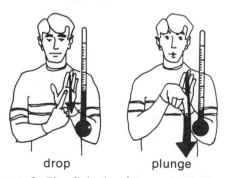

drop   plunge

FIG. **2.** *The distinction between temperature dropping and temperature plunging may be made by distorting the sign so as to provide additional emphasis.*

The right bent "B" hand, fingers pointing downward, may be used instead of the right index finger.

will The pause before this sign establishes the context which makes this the sequel to the previous condition. *Will* is the general American Sign Language gesture for the future: the right hand, palm facing left and fingers pointing forward, is moved forward from the right shoulder across the time line running from left to right in front of the body. Since the future is implied by the preceding context and by the next sign, *begin*, the sign, *will*, which marks the future, is not necessary. Its use is suggested here to add emphasis. The signer may nod his head as he signs *will* to indicate his total agreement with his own prediction.

begin The left hand is held with the fingers extended and the palm facing right. The right index finger is tucked between the index finger and third finger and twisted in a clockwise movement with a twist of the right wrist. Occasionally a counterclockwise twist may be seen as an alternate version of the sign. The field of meaning associated with this sign is very much the same as that associated with the English words, *begin, start*. Subtle shades of meaning can be implied by the way the sign is executed. Signed slowly and cautiously, the sign may mean that something is just barely beginning to happen. Signed forcefully and decisively, the sign may mean that something is certainly happening or about to happen.

snow In the sign for *rain*, "CLAW" hands (bent "5" hands) were streaked downward in front of the face imitating the falling *rain*. Here, the fingers are wiggled as both hands flutter downward, imitating the slowly falling *snow*. The sign may be preceded by the sign for *white:* the fingertips of the thumb and fingers of the right hand are brushed against the chest as the right hand closes its fingers and moves forward from the body. The sign seems to be motivated by feeling a white shirt.

Me want The English word, *me*, is used in the Gloss to suggest that in American Sign Language the first person personal pronoun may be executed by pointing the index finger to the chest, regardless whether the pronoun is the subject or the object of the sentence. There is an initialized sign for *I* which is executed by touching the thumb side of the right "I" hand to the chest. *Want* is signed by draw-

ing the "CLAW" hands (curved "5" hands), palms up, toward the chest of the signer.

disappear The same sign may be used for *disappear* in the sense of slowly vanish from sight and for *melt, dissolve,* in the sense of a physical transformation from a solid to a liquid state. The "5" hands, palms facing, are closed into "A" hands as both hands are moved sideways apart from each other and slightly downward. The speed with which the event is reported to have occurred can be implied by the speed with which the sign is executed.

Every-day This sign is similar to *tomorrow* except that it is repeated several times. For tomorrow the right "A" hand, thumb up, is placed to the right of the cheek, and the thumb is moved forward in an arc with a twist of the wrist. In effect, *tomorrow* and *tomorrow* and *tomorrow* amounts to *every day* (see Fig. 3).

FIG. **3.** *Repetition of a sign may result in a change of meaning, as* **tomorrow, tomorrow, tomorrow** *means* **every day, daily.**

rain, rain, rain The repetition implies an event of long duration.

truly The sign for *true* or *truly* adds emphasis to the statement. It is signed by placing the vertical right index finger near the lips and moving it forward in a decisive movement. Occasionally it may point directly forward in its final position. In an alternate version, the vertical index finger may be rubbed up the lips before moving forward. In general, such additional flourishes add emphasis to the sign.

same, same, same This sign is a fusion of the sign for *same*, which is executed by moving the right "Y" hand back and forth in front of the body as if measuring two things and finding them *the same,* and the sign for *stay,* which is executed by moving one or both "Y" hands forward from the waist across the horizontal time line in front of the body. If something stays as it is and then time passes, the effect is that it is still the same. If it is also something disagreeable, such as prolonged rain, it is *monotonous.* In American Sign Language usage, the meaning *monotonous* is conveyed by moving the two "Y" hands in circles in front of the body so that they come together and then move apart again as if signing *stay, stay, stay* or *same, same, same.* The movements are made laboriously, and a pained facial expression may contribute to the meaning of the sign. The effect of the statement is heightened by the repetition of the previous signs, *every day (tomorrow, tomorrow, tomorrow)* and *rain, rain, rain.*

Me bored The sign for *bored* is executed by "boring" the right index finger with a twisting motion into the side of the bridge of the nose. The little finger may be extended, so as to make the hand configuration more conspicuous, and as the hand is twisted with the index finger pointing at the side of the nose, the palm is flicked toward the face. There are a number of signs executed near the nose or touching the nose. Many of them have a slightly vulgar connotation and should perhaps be avoided in polite society. Among such socially restricted signs are *don't care* (the tip of the index finger is touched to the nose and then flicked away as if casting off worthless mucus), *lousy* (the thumb of the right "3" hand is touched to the tip of the nose and then the right "3" hand is thrown forcefully downward) and *buggy, dirty* (the thumb of the right "3" hand is touched to the nose, and the fingers are curled inward several times). It is no coincidence that the conventional sign for *urinate* is the right "P" hand touched to the tip of the nose. Although they are socially restricted, which implies that it may be inappropriate to use them under some circumstances, they are widely used at times and in places where they are permissible. The American Sign Language user who does not know these signs or does not use them at all has a deficient linguistic repertoire.

Wish The sign for *wish* is derived from the sign for *hungry.* It can also mean *want, long for.* It is executed by drawing the tips of the thumb and fingers of the right "C" hand down the front of the chest. It is a stronger expression than the sign for *want* used previously and described above.

sky The sign for *sky* traces the vault of the heavens over the earth with both hands, palms down. This is one of very few signs that are executed above the level of the head of the signer.

blue Some of the signs for colors involve touching a place on the body where an example of that color may be found, such as *red* on the lips, *black* on the right eyebrow, and *white* on the shirt. *Blue, green, yellow,* and *purple* are signed by twisting the right hand at the wrist several times as the right hand forms the first letter of the English name for each color. The sign can be intensified by moving it off to the right as the hand is shaken to suggest *deep blue, deep purple,* etc. The sequence, sky blue, is found very frequently in American Sign Language. First the noun is named, and then the descriptive adjective is added.

sunshine This is a compound sign. First a circle is traced in the sky, representing the sun, and then the right hand changes from an "O" configuration to a "5" configuration, palm down, representing the rays of the sun beaming downward, as the hand is moved downward in front of the signer.

warm The sign for *warm* may be derived from the warmth of the human breath. The "A" hand, thumb up, is placed in front of the mouth and then opened slowly to the "5" position as it is moved upward and away from the mouth. A related sign, *hot,* begins with the palm of the "CLAW" hand (bent "5" hand) held in front of the mouth and then turns the hand quickly away so that the palm faces outward. Again, the sequence is noun-adjective.

True The head may be nodded slightly as the sign for *true* is executed, implying as-

6

sent, even if grudgingly given. The lips may be pinched together to indicate unwilling assent.

know The fingertips of the right hand are tapped to the forehead several times. In an alternate form of the sign, the fingertips of the right hand are pressed against the forehead.

need rain The order in which these two signs are executed is a matter of choice. *Rain* might be signed first in order to indicate the subject of the discourse. In that case, *need* would have to be parsed as if it were a participial construction, *is needed*. If *need* is signed first, some other subject, such as *we*, would be likely to be understood.

for The horizontal right index finger is placed near the forehead with the fingertips toward or touching the forehead in the initial position. It is turned outward with a twist of the right wrist so that the fingertip faces outward. This sign translates the French *pour*. It is one of the few signs that have come down to the present in American Sign Language usage intact from the French model developed by the Abbe de l'Epee. Since it was originally developed as a Sign Language equivalent for *pour*, its field of meaning is comparable to the French vocable. Primarily it expresses *purpose*. In this context, it means *for* in the sense of *for the benefit of, for the purpose of aiding* the farmers.

farmer This is a compound sign: *farm + the person marker*. The sign for *the person marker* is derived from the sign for *person:* the two hands, palms facing, trace the outline of a human figure in front or off to the side of the signer. To indicate *the person marker* as the suffix of another sign, the two hands are drawn downward at the sides of the signer's body immediately after executing the sign to which it is attached. It is tempting to consider *the person marker* in American Sign Language as the equivalent of the suffix, *-er*, in English. This, however, over-states the extent to which the usages are similar. In English, a *jail* and a *prison* are the same thing, and in American Sign Language they are signed the same way. But in English, a *jailor* and a *prisoner* are on

opposite sides of the bars. The American Sign Language sign for *jail + the person marker* or *prison + the person marker* always means *prisoner*.

their The open palm is the possessive marker in American Sign Language. In this case, it is directed outward in a sweeping movement that encompasses a large enough region to imply the plural for *farmer*.

grow area The sign for *grow* is ordinarily a verb, but this does not mean that it cannot be used as a noun or an adjective. In American Sign Language there is no specific sign for *crops*. *Grow area* is suggested as a way to indicate the physical reality of growing things, that is, *crops*. Another way to indicate the noun, *crops*, rather than the verb, *grow,* is to repeat the sign for *grow* as the hands move from left to right across the front of the body.

Rain disappear This is a conditional clause. It is not marked by a special sign as would be the case in English (*If the rain disappears*), but the meaning is clear. A slight pause after *disappear* can insure that the conditional aspect of the statement is understood.

all The signer has a choice here of either executing the traditional sign for *all* or of sweeping the right hand across the *crops* which have just been localized in front of him and to the right as the right hand fingerspells *A L L.*

dry The right "X" hand is drawn from left to right across the mouth as if wiping parched lips. The same sign executed on the forehead means *hot* or *summer*. The left index finger may point to the imaginary crops as the right hand executes *dry*.

wither This is an example of reversing the meaning of a sign by reversing its movement (see Fig. 4). The sign for *grow* is made by thrusting the fingers of the right hand up through the left "O" hand as the right hand opens into a "5" position. To sign *wither* or *shrivel*, the right "5" hand is drawn slowly back into the left "0" hand. If one wished to press the issue further, the right hand could sweep across the *crops* again, this time executing the sign for *die*, that is, the right hand is held, palm up, and then turned over with a twist of the wrist. The facial expression may be contorted so as to show an appropriate reaction to everything withering and dying.

grow   wither

FIG. 4. *An antonym may be indicated by reversing the movement of a sign.*

Idea The right "I" hand is hooked upward in an arc from the forehead. The accompanying facial expression indicates a change of mood. The meaning is roughly equivalent to the English, "I have an idea." As an alternative, there is another natural, expressive gesture which might be used to attract attention to the suggestion that is to follow: the right index finger can be raised up in the air as if to say, *Wait!*

All-night The right hand is moved slowly down and under the horizon established by the horizontal left forearm, and slowly raised again to a horizontal position parallel with the left arm. The slow, sweeping movement implies an event that is continuous, that is, *all night.*

morning stop The left arm again represents the horizon, but this time the sun comes up in the morning from underneath the forearm.

Why not? *Why* is an interrogative in American Sign Language, and an additional marker, such as a question mark, is not needed to designate this as a question. *Why* is signed by holding the right hand so that the palm is toward the forehead. The hand is brought forward from the forehead with the palm still facing the signer, but the hand configuration changes to a "Y" hand. *Not* would probably be signed here with

the right thumb jerked out from under the chin in an abrupt gesture. In fact, in ordinary usage, *why not* is often elided so that the *why* is barely visible. All that is seen is the initial position for *Why,* and the right hand moves immediately to the execution of *not.* Arched eyebrows and an expectant posture may also serve to mark the item as a question. The rhythm of the three clusters here is important. Between each there is an appropriate pause, and after the last one, the muscle tone and body stance should imply special emphasis. Notice that each of the three can be executed more quickly than the previous one. *All night* takes some time to execute because of the sweeping gesture. *Morning stop* still takes a little time because the hands have to move from the final position for *morning* to the initial position for *stop* before the sign can be completed. But *Why not* is signed very quickly in front of the face. Such changes in tempo serve to enhance the literary quality of American Sign Language utterances and to make them interesting for a receiver.

Fridays The sign for Friday is an initialized sign: the right "F" hand makes a small circle in front of the right shoulder. The other days of the week (except *Sunday*) are signed similarly. *Thursday* includes the "H"

Friday   Fridays

Monday
Mondays

FIG. 5. *A downward movement attached to a sign for one of the days of the week implies a customary or habitual action.*

8

configuration to distinguish it from *Tuesday*. If the right hand is dragged downward in front of the body after the sign is executed, the meaning becomes *Fridays* or *every Friday* (see Fig. 5). The sign does not imply that there are no exceptions, but it indicates what is customary. It is comparable to the English expression, *Sundays people go to church*.

nice The same sign that means *clean* in other contexts may also be used for *nice,* speaking of the weather. Note that the same kind of rhetorical structure is again present for three succinct clusters of signs. Each cluster has two signs, the clusters are punctuated by pauses, and each set ends in an abrupt question, *Why not?*

Me rule, make fine This statement is clearly a conditional sentence. The sign for *make* may also mean *fix*, and either connotation is appropriate here. *Fine* is a very common expression in American Sign Language. It is the typical answer to the question, "How are you?" It can also mean *polite*. The sign can be executed in a subdued manner, tapping the thumb of the right "5" hand to the chest, or in a flamboyant manner, touching the thumb of the right "5" hand to the chest and then throwing it forward and outward from the body. The present context calls for a bit of emphasis, but perhaps not as vigorous as the "flamboyant" manner suggested above. In this case the facial expression might carry most of the emphasis by appearing very smug and self satisfied as the thumb of the right "5" hand is tapped repeatedly to the chest.

Me decide The smug expression adopted for *fine* would be maintained for the initial comment here, as if the signer had divine or at least superhuman power to make decisions with regard to the weather. *Decide* is a compound, *think* plus a derivative of *judge*. In *judge* the "F" hands are moved up and down alternately (and indecisively) in front of the chest. In *decide* the "F" hands are brought down forcibly to a full stop.

Saturday Sunday The conjunction, *and* is unnecessary here. The hands could be moved downward, as mentioned previ-

ously, to indicate customary or habitual performance. But the next sign, *always,* makes that unnecessary and, as a matter of fact, is a little stronger, implying that there will be no exceptions.

always The right index finger, pointing forward, makes a clockwise circle at the right side of the body.

pleasant This sign is executed by gently fanning the face with the palms of both hands, palms back, as the hands are bent at the knuckles and held at the side of the head. The same sign also means *cool*. An alternate version wiggles the fingers as the hands are held in the same location as if to feel the breezes blowing between them. Generally the sign refers to *pleasant weather*, although it may be used metaphorically to refer to other pleasant events or circumstances.

Mondays The right hand drags the "M" downward to imply a habitual or characteristic action, as in *Fridays* above. In addition, the sign may be dislocated, either by executing it with the left hand or by signing it off to the right. This dislocation serves a double purpose. First, it helps to differentiate *Mondays* from *Saturdays* and *Sundays,* which are signed in their usual location. Secondly, it allows *phooey* to be aimed at the location established for *Mondays,* which makes clear the connection between the expletive and the day of the week for which it is intended. Such spatial organization of signs serves to connect signs with one another in longer units, and, therefore, constitutes an important syntactic feature of American Sign Language.

Phooey! This is a natural gesture; the right hand, palm out, is flung away from the body in the general direction of the object of disgust in an emphatic put down. Directed toward a person, the sign may serve as a rough translation of *Go to hell*. It is a strong sign, and it is socially restricted, although if it is executed without much vigor and without a person as the object, it is not necessarily offensive.

Let rain *Let* corresponds in general to the English *permit, allow*. It resembles somewhat a natural gesture in which the hands are moved forward from the body as if to say, "Go ahead, go." In the present context the sign would probably be executed off to the side of the body, off in the general direction of the despised *Monday,* and the head could be turned away, not even looking in that direction, as if to suggest by looking away that one is completely unconcerned about the rain that is falling on Monday. Such use of the direction of the line of vision is an important feature of American Sign Language usage, and it has not been studied carefully by psycholinguists. In particular, some of the important questions that need to be considered about the gaze of the signer are the following: Is the signer maintaining close eye contact with the receiver? Is eye contact with the receiver deliberately being avoided? Is the signer looking intently at some place where an item has previously been localized? Does the looking behavior of the sender add important information about the affective state of the signer or the feelings that he has about the subject matter? When he has completed his statement, does the signer then establish or maintain eye contact with the receiver, as if awaiting a response, or does he break it off, effectively terminating the conversation? Mastery of American Sign Language requires also mastery of one's line of vision as an important aspect of the communicative act.

VOCABULARY

Note: In these Vocabulary listings, HH refers to *Sign Language Flash Cards* by Harry W. Hoemann & Shirley A. Hoemann, and TO refers to *A Basic Course in Manual Communication* by T. J. O'Rourke. Both of these publications are available from the National Association of the Deaf, 814 Thayer Ave., Silver Spring, MD 20910.

1. after while (HH-262, TO-531)
2. a little while ago (HH-262)
3. all (HH-494, TO-193)
4. all night (HH-308, TO-187)
5. allow (TO-348)
6. always (HH 370, TO-83)
7. and (HH-46, TO-239)
8. area (see text)
9. become (HH-28, TO-280)
10. begin (HH-124, TO-458)
11. black (HH-284, TO-88)
12. blow (see text)
13. blue (HH-353, TO-437)
14. bored (see text)
15. buggy (HH-113)
16. change (HH-484, TO-663)
17. clean (HH-112, TO-48)
18. cool (HH-189)
19. crops (see text)
20. decide (HH-147, TO-558)
21. deep blue (HH-353)
22. die (HH-241)
23. dirty (HH-113)
24. disappear (HH-481, TO-245)
25. dissolve (HH-481, TO-245)
26. don't care (HH-102)
27. doubt (HH-338, TO-157)
28. drop (see text)
29. dry (HH-67, TO-632)
30. East (HH-161, TO-474)
31. every day (HH-104, TO-90)
32. farm (HH-129)
33. farmer (HH-129)
34. fine (HH-444, TO-135)
35. fix (HH-210, TO-298)
36. for (HH-404, TO-18)
37. forget (HH-120, TO-517)
38. Fridays (HH-328, TO-267)
39. from (HH-16, TO-33)
40. go to hell (see text)
41. green (HH-353, TO-434)
42. grow (HH-364, TO-487)
43. happen (HH-174, TO-228)
44. hot (HH-498, TO-136)
45. hungry (HH-165, TO-404)
46. idea (HH-134, TO-418)
47. ignorant (HH-236, TO-213)
48. jail (TO-264)
49. judge (HH-306, TO-559)
50. know (HH-14, TO-206)
51. later (HH-262, TO-531)
52. law (HH-287, TO-522)
53. left (HH-161)
54. let (TO-348)
55. long for (HH-165, TO-404)
56. lousy (HH-398)
57. make (HH-210, TO-298)
58. maybe (HH-19, TO-51)
59. me (HH-192, TO-2)
60. melt (HH-481, TO-245)
61. Mondays (HH-328, TO-267)
62. monotonous (HH-278)
63. morning (HH-228, TO-183)
64. multiply (HH-132, TO-301)
65. need (HH-62, TO-628)
66. nice (HH-112, TO-48)
67. North (HH-161, TO-474)
68. not (HH-249, TO-44)
69. now (HH-2, TO-47)
70. once upon a time (HH-174, TO-228)
71. permit (TO-348)
72. person marker (HH-18, TO-426)
73. phooey (see text)
74. pleasant (HH-189)
75. plunge (see text)
76. polite (HH-444, TO-134)
77. previously (HH-262)
78. prison (TO-264)
79. prisoner (TO-264)

80. purple (HH-353, TO-439)
81. purpose (HH-404, TO-18)
82. rain (HH-9, TO-251)
83. red (HH-425, TO-436)
84. right (HH-161)
85. rule (HH-409)
86. same (see text)
87. Saturday (HH-328, TO-267)
88. Saturdays (HH-328, TO-267)
89. shrivel (see text)
90. sky (HH-186)
91. snow (HH-9, TO-250)
92. south (HH-161, TO-474)
93. start (HH-124, TO-458)
94. stay (HH-278, TO-647)
95. stop (HH-430, TO-54)
96. stupid (HH-389, TO-588)
97. summer (HH-441. TO-634)
98. Sunday (HH-322, TO-266)
99. sunshine (HH-456)
100. teach (HH-123, TO-253)
101. temperature (see text)

102. their (HH-469)
103. think (HH-226, TO-79)
104. tomorrow (HH-104, TO-92)
105. true (HH-291, TO-219)
106. truly (HH-291, TO-219)
107. urinate (HH-102)
108. wait! (see text)
109. want (HH-448, TO-173)
110. warm (HH-356, TO-137)
111. West (HH-161, TO-474)
112. which (HH-333, TO-130)
113. white (HH-459, TO-238)
114. why? (HH-8, TO-16)
115. will (HH-360, TO-201)
116. wind (see text)
117. wise (HH-21, TO-635)
118. wish (HH-165, TO-404)
119. wither (see text)
120. worse (TO-301)
121. yellow (HH-353, TO-438)
122. you (HH-403, TO-3)

EXERCISES

Sign the following sentences and provide an English translation.

1. Grow grow area now dry, yellow; need rain; make area green.

2. Now morning wind change, become warm; snow area melt.

3. Rain Saturday, boring; rain Sunday, worse.

4. Sky truly black, will rain, me know.

5. You not think; you stupid; you don't care; why?

6. Jail you Friday, Saturday, which?

7. All night rain, now stop; maybe later pleasant.

8. Farm truly dry; need rain.

9. Every-day you teach, every-day me forget. why me forget? Me don't-care.

10. You phooey me; what for? Not polite; stop.

Lesson Two

ENGLISH ORIGINAL

Summer Camp

This year my 16-year-old daughter spent her first summer away from home. She was in a work-study camp in North Carolina. I have never been there, but I know about where it is. It is near the South Carolina border, not far from the South Carolina School for the Deaf. My daughter flew down from Ohio at the beginning of summer. When the season was over, she rode with some friends to Washington, D.C., where I had been attending the Seventh World Congress. When she arrived in Washington she was all excited about her experiences at camp. She said her teacher was really strict and forced her to study hard, but I find that hard to believe. I could see that she enjoyed the whole experience. Already she has said she wants to go back next year. We spent two days in Washington. I wanted to see some people at Gallaudet College, and she wanted to do some sight seeing. We were satisfied to limit our stay in Washington to two days. After that we had enough. We were ready to go home.

SIGN LANGUAGE GLOSS

Summer C-A-M-P

Now year my daughter old sixteen first time summer live away home. Go to C-A-M-P, work study C-A-M-P, in N.C. Me there never, but area where? me know. Near line S.C. near S. C. institution. C-A-M-P, institution, not far, near. Ago summer begin, daughter fly there from O-H-I-O. C-A-M-P finish, group, her friend, drive Washington, person ride-along. Me there same time. Why? Seventh World Congress. Daughter arrive Washington, truly excited from experiences ago C-A-M-P. She explain, teacher strict, force study, study, hard. Me doubt. Can see, she enjoy all summer. Finish say next year want again go there. We-two stay in Washington two day. Me want see there there there people Gallaudet College, daughter want see there there there around Washington. We satisfied limit two day stay Washington. She finish, me finish, enough. We-two ready go home.

GRAMMATICAL NOTES

Now year To sign *now*, both hands, palms up, are brought downward in front of the body to a full stop in front of the waist. "Y" hands may be used. The sign for *now* is often used as a time marker for the present tense. *Now + day =today. Now + week = this week.* By the same token, *now + year = this year.* To avoid any ambiguity and to insure that the adverb, *now,* is taken as modifying the following noun, *year,* rather than as a connective introducing a new thought, the location of the sign may be shifted slightly closer to the body, and the shoulders hunched slightly. The net effect of both of those modifications is to have the sign *now* executed almost exactly where the sign for *year* is about to be executed. Also, there is no pause between *now* and *year.* The sign for *year* is executed by circling the right fist around the left, with the right fist resting on top of the left in the final position. The sign is said to be derived from the revolution of the earth around the sun.

my daughter The open palm is the possessive marker in American Sign Language. Placed against the signer's chest, it means *my* or *mine.* Directed outward it may mean *your, his, her, hers,* or *its.* If it is directed outward several times, it becomes the plural, *your, their, theirs.* The first person plural, *our,* is indicated by moving the hand from the right to the left shoulder with the palm facing the body all the time. *Daughter* is a compound, comprised of the sign for *girl* or *female* followed by the sign for *baby. Girl, female* is signed by stroking the thumb of the right "A" hand down the right cheek or jaw. As with compounds generally, the elements are not executed exactly as they would be if they were used in their literal sense. In the present case, *baby* is not rocked back and forth. Instead, the right arm is dropped downward along the horizontal left arm so as to barely make contact with it. The sign for *son* is also a compound, *man* or *male + baby.*

old sixteen The order of the signs here would probably be reversed compared to English. It is a general rule in American

Sign Language that one must first state what it is he is talking about before he begins to talk about it. This rule may have evolved from the reliance of Sign Languages on a visual channel. In any case, it is less ambiguous to raise the issue of age first and then announce *sixteen* rather than to first state the numeral and then explain what it was that was counted so as to yield the number. *Old* is motivated by a *beard:* The right "C" or "O" hand makes a waving movement downward from the chin. *Sixteen* may be signed by simply rubbing the thumb along the inside edge of the little finger as the remaining three fingers are held upright. This resembles the sign, *six,* except that for *six* the thumb tip is tapped to the tip of the little finger. These slight differences in contact between *six* and *sixteen* are sufficient, because the rubbing movement accompanying *sixteen* will also result in some movement of the fourth and perhaps the third fingers of the hand as well. Some manuals suggest that *sixteen* should be signed by first presenting the numeral *ten,* the upraised thumb, and then, with a twist of the wrist, the numeral *six.* This longer form is sometimes seen,

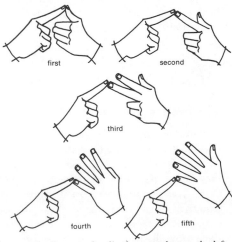

first   second

third

fourth   fifth

FIG. 6. *One set of ordinal numerals uses the left hand to indicate the numeral as the right index finger touches the thumb or one of the fingers of the left.*

but numerals are used so frequently among deaf persons that regional variations are common, and the student of American Sign Language will have to be alert to whatever practice is found among the deaf people with whom he expects to associate.

first time One set of ordinal numerals uses the fingers of the left hand as the primary source of information, as they are struck by the index finger of the right hand. *First* is signed by striking the right index finger against the upraised left thumb. For *second,* the left hand is held, palm up, with the thumb and index finger extended, and the right index finger is struck downward against the left index finger. For *third* the left hand is held the same way but with the numeral *three* exposed, and the right index finger strikes the middle finger of the left hand. *Fourth* tucks the thumb into the left palm, exposing the four fingers, and the right index finger is struck against the little finger of the left hand. It should be noted that *first* involves a different direction of movement than *second, third,* and *fourth.* In the latter three, the right index finger is moved downward as the left hand is held with the palm up. In *first* the thumb is presented up, and the right index finger moves toward the left so as to strike the right fingertip against the left thumb tip (see Fig. 6). *Time* may be signed in one of two ways. Either the right index fingertip is touched to the back of the left wrist, where a watch is likely to be worn, or the left hand is turned to face the right, fingertips pointing upward, and the right "T" hand traces a circle on the left palm, as if traversing the 60 minutes of the hour on a clock. The latter sign is somewhat more likely to be used for a duration of time, while the former is likely to be associated with a certain time on the clock. The present context permits either sign.

summer The right "X" hand is scraped from left to right across the forehead. The sign may be derived from wiping perspiration from the brow (see Fig. 7). In other contexts, the same sign may mean *hot* or *hard work.* The signs for two of the other seasons of the year also have other mean-

ings. *Spring* may also mean *grow,* and *winter* may also mean *cold* (see Fig. 8).

FIG. **7.** *The sign for* **Summer** *may be derived from wiping perspiration from the brow.*

FIG. **8.** *The sign for* **Winter** *also means* **cold.**

live away home To sign *live,* both fists are rubbed upward on the chest. "L" hands may be used. *Away* is simply a natural gesture; the right hand, palm down, is waved off at the distance as if indicating some distant area. A similar gesture executed forcefully may mean *go away. Home* touches the fingertips of the "AND" hand to the mouth and to the cheek. The hand may be opened as the fingertips touch the cheek. This sign is said to be derived from the fact that home is where one eats and sleeps. *Live away home* is signed as a group without any hesitation or pause between the signs. The emphasis in the phrase is on the sign

15

away. That emphasis might be indicated in a variety of ways. The head may be raised slightly as the sign for *away* is executed, eye contact may be established with the receiver just as the sign *away* is executed, the signer may squint or puff out his cheeks as he signs *away* to highlight that sign in comparison with the others, or the signer may draw his body up to a taller height as he signs *away.* The student of American Sign Language should be a careful observer of deaf persons and their Sign Language usage so that these subtle, but very effective, devices for adding appropriate emphasis are mastered.

Go to C-A-M-P *Go* may be signed by simply moving the upraised right index finger away from the body. It would be appropriate to move it off in the same direction where *away* has just been signed. In fact, for the sake of subsequent referencing, it is important that the location of this camp be established relative to the signer's body. Home may be close to the body, while the camp may be off at an angle toward the right. *To* is signed by touching the tip of the right index finger to the tip of the left index finger. It could be omitted here, since *Go camp* is unambiguous. *C-A-M-P* is likely to be fingerspelled. One could perhaps repeat the sign for *tent* several times, and that is listed in some manuals as a sign for *camp,* but the fact is that many camps have cabins rather than tents, and fingerspelling is resorted to rather frequently by deaf persons when they know an English word that has the precise meaning they wish to convey.

work study C-A-M-P *Work* is signed by striking the wrist of the right fist against the wrist of the left fist several times. *Study* is signed in two ways. In both versions the left palm is turned up, as if presenting what is to be studied. In one version the right hand is held with the fingers clustered together, and the fingers are then flicked at the left palm as the hand is moved toward the left palm repeatedly. In the other version, the right "5" hand is held with the fingers pointing toward the left palm, and they are wiggled for a time

as the right hand is held in that orientation toward the left. Again, *C-A-M-P* is fingerspelled. This is a parenthetical expression, defining the kind of camp that the daughter attended. Since it is an explanation designed especially to clarify a point for the receiver, it is likely that the sender would establish eye contact with the receiver as this expression is signed. Prior to that the signer may have been looking off in the direction where he has localized the camp, as if he were thinking about it. Such use of the direction of the line of vision is an important feature of sign language. It may be used during the time that a particular referent is being localized, to insure that the receiver has ample opportunity to assimilate the locations that are being established. Subsequently, a glance in that direction may take the place of a pronoun in English or of pointing in that direction in Sign Language. By breaking eye contact with the location of the camp and establishing eye contact with the receiver, rapport is temporarily enhanced, and that is important if some kind of explanatory information is being added for the receiver's benefit.

in N C *In* is signed by tucking the fingertips of the right "AND" hand into the opening of the left "O" hand. Many of the states of the United States are indicated by their common abbreviations. Thus, *N-C* is used for *North Carolina. U-S* is used for the *United States.*

Me there never. *Me* is signed by touching the tip of the right index finger to the signer's chest. *There* is signed by simply pointing with the right index finger to the location established for the camp. Since these two signs combined have the effect of pointing first to the signer and then to the location for the camp, a back translation from the American Sign Language version to English may read, literally, "Me go there never" or "I have never gone there." *Never* waves the right hand, palm turned out, back and forth several times as the hand moves downward in front of the signer's body. It may be derived from *no* or *don't,* which involves lateral movements of both hands with the palms turned outward.

but The crossed index fingers are drawn apart in an abrupt movement. In other contexts the sign may mean *different, on the contrary*. Since this sign introduces a change of viewpoint, the signer is likely to signal this with a change in facial expression.

area where? Again, the location of the camp relative to the signer's body is important for the execution of this phrase. For *area,* the right hand, palm down, is moved around in the general direction or location of the camp. Then the question, *where?* is added, as the right index finger is waggled back and forth as it addresses the location of the camp. A questioning facial expression marks the *where* as a question.

Me know *Me* is signed as indicated previously. For *know* the index fingers of the right hand are tapped to the forehead. Since some assurance is implied by the sender that even though he has never been to the camp he feels comfortable about his knowledge about where it is, additional cues might accompany the sign as it is executed. For example, the signer might nod his head as he taps the fingertips of the right hand to his forehead.

Near line S C The sign order is optional here. One might prefer to sign *S C line* (border) and then make the sign *near*. The sign for *near* uses the bent left hand as a point of reference and moves the bent right hand close to it. The bent right hand may approach the left from a distance away from the body and come *near* or *close* from that direction, or the right hand may begin close to the body and approach the left hand from that direction. In this case, the camp is located some distance away from where the signer is presumed to be as he is telling the story, so it is unlikely that the right hand would approach the left from a distance as if coming closer to the signer. In fact, the context practically requires that the left hand be removed some distance from the body before the right hand approaches it, since the left hand really represents the South Carolina border. Moreover, the camp has already been localized some distance from the signer's body. Under these kinds of circumstances, a sign may be dislocated from its ordinary place of execution and be signed in a location that takes into account the way in which the signer has localized absent referents for subsequent discussion. South Carolina is indicated by its common abbreviation, *S C. Line* is signed by touching the tips of the little fingers together and then drawing them apart. The same sign in other contexts may mean *thread* or *string*. Here it implies a *boundary line or border*.

Near S C institution Again, *near* is likely to be displaced from its ordinary location in front of the body and be signed, instead, in the general area where the camp has been localized relative to the signer (see Fig. 9). *Institution* is signed by striking the right "I" hand to the top of the left "I" hand several times. In American Sign Language, when the term *institution* is used without further clarification, it is a residential school for the deaf that is being referenced. In this case it is the South Carolina School for the Deaf, located in Spartanburg, S.C.

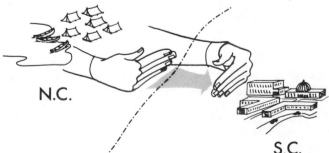

N.C.

S.C.

FIG. 9. *The sign for* **near** *may be displaced from its ordinary place of execution so as to accommodate to the locations established for the summer camp and the South Carolina School for the Deaf.*

C-A-M-P institution not far, near Here the use of localization can provide a clear and effective strategy for indicating the relationship between the summer camp and the deaf school. There are a couple of options. The most straightforward is to simply spell *C-A-M-P* directly over the area where the camp has been localized, then to sign *institution* also some distance from the body and near the camp, and then to sign *not* and *far,* with the thumbs of the two hands executing *far* spanning the distance between the locations established for the *camp* and the *deaf school.* A second possibility is to point at the location of the camp with the left hand while spelling *C-A-M-P* with the right, then sign *institution* and point to a location close to the one established for the camp, and then proceed with *not far,* again executing the sign for *far* between the locations to which the signer has pointed. *Not* is signed by bumping the underside of the chin with the tip of the right thumb as the right "A" hand, thumb up, is moved forward from the chest. *Far* uses both thumb-up "A" hands. The left one provides a point of reference, and the right one is moved away from the left and away from the signer's body to indicate some distance. *Far away* would be indicated by holding the left hand, thumb up, near the chest, and the right hand would be placed near it and then moved far off to the front and right from the body. Since the execution of the sign itself implies some distance, the present translation suggests that it be followed by the sign *near,* so as to indicate the true nature of the situation. Thus, *C-A-M-P* (located there) *institution* (located there) *not far* (with *far* spanning the distance between them) *near* (with the right and left hands originating at each appropriate location and moving toward each other so as to indicate proximity).

Ago summer begin Until now, there has been no need for a temporal frame of reference for the narrative. The signer is simply discussing his daughter's first summer away from home. No past or future events have been mentioned. Now, however, a past event is introduced, namely, a plane flight which took place at the beginning of the summer. A past marker is appropriate here to indicate that this is a past event. The right hand is moved back over the right shoulder one or more times. *Summer* is signed as indicated previously. *Begin* is signed by twisting the right index finger with a twist of the wrist as it is tucked between the index and middle fingers of the left hand.

Daughter fly there from O-H-I-O *Daughter* is signed as indicated previously. *Fly* is signed the same as the noun, *airplane.* The thumb and little finger indicate the wings as the index finger indicates the body of the aircraft. The hand is moved off to the location of the summer camp. Since the final destination is indicated by the direction of movement of the sign toward the localized summer camp, the pointing gesture for *there* is optional. *From* is signed by holding the left index finger extended as a point of reference and by pulling the hooked right index finger (the right "X" hand) away from it, typically toward the signer's body. In this case, that is entirely appropriate, because Ohio is apparently home, and after the execution of *from* the right hand can be left close to the chest of the signer to spell *O-H-I-O.*

C-A-M-P finish Again, *C-A-M-P* is fingerspelled. *Finish* is signed by holding both "5" hands, palms up, in front of the body, and flicking them over abruptly. One hand may be used instead of two.

group her friend One way to pluralize a noun in American Sign Language is to add the sign for *group* either before or after the noun. In the present case, some of the daughter's friends drove to Washington, D.C. To indicate that it was more than one friend, the sign for *group* is indicated first, and then the *group* is defined as comprised of friends. *Group* is signed by enclosing an imaginary group with both hands, palms facing. *Her* uses the possessive marker; the open palm is directed outward, probably in the direction of the camp. If there is any concern over ambiguity here, the sign for *daughter* may be repeated and then followed immediately by the sign *her. Friend* is signed by locking the curved index fingers together first in one direction and then the other.

drive Washington It is important that Washington be localized somewhere else than either Ohio (close to the body) or the summer camp at North Carolina (off at an angle to the right). The best available space is off at an angle to the left. This location can be established immediately with the introduction of the verb, *drive*. It can be executed off to the left, and then the sign for *Washington* can follow and reflect the localization of the city for the purposes of this narrative. *Drive* imitates the holding of a steering wheel. The same sign may also mean *car, automobile*. *Washington* is signed by touching the right "W" to the right shoulder and then circling the "W" in front of the right shoulder. In this case the circle might be executed somewhat off to the left, reflecting the direction that the sign for *drive* took. In addition, the left index finger may point off to the left as the sign for Washington is executed.

person ride-along The reference to the daughter may be accomplished in one of three ways. One way is to simply point to the location of the summer camp. If there is any concern about ambiguity, the sign for *person* may be used. An even more explicit reference would be to repeat the sign for *daughter,* but that is probably unnecessary. *Ride-along* is signed by tucking the

index and middle fingers of the right hand in the left "O" hand, and then moving both hands in the same direction as was followed by drive, ending at the location that has been established for Washington, D.C.

Me there same time *Me* is signed as before. The advantage to localizing Washington off to the left is immediately apparent when the sign for *there* is executed. By keeping the locations of the camp and Washington distinctively separate, pointing to either one of them unambiguously references either the one or the other (see Fig. 10). In this case, *there* means Washington, D.C., so the index finger is pointed off to the left. *Same* is signed by laying both index fingers parallel to each other and touching in a horizontal plane with the fingers pointing forward. The fingers may be touched together several times. Or the right "Y" hand, palm down, may move back and forth between the signer's body and the location established for Washington, D.C. *Time* would probably be signed by touching the back of the left wrist with the tip of the right index finger.

Why? Causal clauses are rare in American Sign Language. The easiest way to indicate a cause or a reason is to put the question in the mind of the receiver by asking it. Once the signer has asked "Why?" he may proceed to give the answer. Since this is a rapport building device, eye contact with the receiver is likely.

FIG. 10. *The localization of Washington relative to the signer and the summer camp makes a directional sign unambiguous.*

first   second   third

FIG. 11. *One set of ordinal numerals hooks the numerals in front of the right shoulder.*

Seventh World Congress Another series of ordinal numerals uses a hooking movement brought about by a twist of the wrist executed in front of the right shoulder (see Fig. 11). Thus, the numeral *seven* means nothing else than *seven* as long as it is presented without any special modulation. But if the wrist is twisted so that the numeral hooks downward in the shape of a "J," it means *seventh*. In this way the ordinal numerals *first* through *ninth* may be executed. *World* is signed similarly to *year* except that the letter "W" is formed on the right hand or on both hands as the right hand revolves around the left. For *Congress* the right "C" hand is touched first to the right shoulder and then to the left shoulder. The Seventh World Congress was held in Washington, D.C., during the latter part of July and early August, 1975.

Daughter arrive Washington *Daughter* and *Washington* are signed as indicated previously. *Arrive* uses the left hand, palm up, as a point of contact. The right hand, palm up, is brought up, forward, and then down so that the back of the right hand lands in the palm of the left. The relative adverb, *when,* is unnecessary here. All that is needed for the sense of the text is that the daughter's arrival be acknowledged.

truly excited *Truly* is an emphasis marker in American Sign Language. It can mean some of the same things as *very, really, surely. Excited* is signed by alternately striking the tips of the middle fingers of the right and left hands against the body as the hands are brought upward along the body with twists of the wrists. An alternate version brings both hands up once simultaneously with a twist of both wrists, the tips of the middle fingers grazing the chest on the way past. The latter sign may also mean *thrilled.*

from experiences The English idiom requires the preposition *about* with the verbs *excited* and *thrilled.* In some cases, the preposition *over* might be used. In American Sign Language neither of these choices would be likely, since the relational aspects of the hands convey some nuance of the meaning of the preposition. *From* fits the occasion better, since it is the memories of the summer taken with her *from* the camp that provide grounds for the daughter's excitement. *Experience* is signed by placing the right "5" hand at the side of the head and moving it off to the right as the fingertips close into the "AND" hand configuration. The sign suggests taking something from the mind. The movement may be repeated several times. Since the experience has to do with the camp and not with Washington, D.C., the signer may anticipate the subsequent reference to the camp by a glance toward the location that has been established for it. Such use of eye movement to reference people, places, or things that have been localized relative to the signer's body constitutes an important feature of American Sign Language usage and an important communication skill to be acquired. It is probably acquired by deaf children as an extension of their early use of pointing to various features of their environment so as to reference them. At first, young deaf children are very limited in their ability to reference items in their environments. They can reference only people or things that are immediately present, where they can point to them. But by the time deaf children are seven to eight years old, they may point to the blackboard to reference the teacher even when the teacher is out of the room. Thus, a location where an item is customarily found becomes the symbol for the referent, and by pointing to the location, the absent referent is indicated. Later, as the children acquire additional skills at dramatization, and are able to coordinate a variety of perspectives, they are able to establish locations for absent referents in the physical space that surrounds their bodies. Then, they may refer to these absent referents either by pointing to these locations or by simply glancing in their direction.

20

ago C-A-M-P The American Sign Language translation may need a past marker here to make it plain that the excitement is a carry-over effect from the previous summer camp. *Camp* is fingerspelled.

She explain Now the daughter is no longer at the camp, so it will not work to point to the summer camp's location to reference her. Instead, if pointing is to be used, it will have to be in the direction of Washington, D.C. Again, if in doubt, the noun, *daughter,* may be repeated. *Explain* is signed by bringing the thumbs and index fingers of both hands together in front of the body so that they can make contact with each other and then be brought apart again repeatedly. The sign may be derived from the notion of spinning yarn. The other fingers may be extended, as in "F" hands, or they may be clenched into fists, so that the resulting hand configuration used would be "G" hands. "F" hands are used for the related signs, *interpret* and *describe.* In these signs, the "F" hands are held with the thumb tips and index fingertips in contact and the hands are held near one another. For *describe* they are moved alternately forward and backward. For *interpret* the wrists are twisted alternately in opposite directions.

Teacher strict *Teach* brings the hands forward from the temples, beginning as "5" hands, palms facing, and ending with the hands in the "AND" configuration. The *person marker* is signed by bringing both hands, palms near and facing the body, downward alongside the body. A sidelong glance in the direction of the location of the summer camp may assist in clarifying that the narrative is now going back to something that is associated with the camp rather than with Washington, D.C. *Strict* is signed by striking the knuckles of the bent "H" hand against the bridge of the nose.

Force study study hard *Force* is signed by shoving the right "C" hand forward and over the left wrist with a forceful gesture. *Study* is signed as indicated previously. The sign is repeated for emphasis. *Hard* uses the same hand configuration as *strict.* This time it is struck downward against the back of the left fist.

Me doubt *Me* is signed as before. For *doubt* the fingers of the right "V" hand are pointed to the eyes, and the fingers are curled inward several times with an appropriately skeptical facial expression. There is another sign for *doubt:* the fists of both hands are moved up and down alternately in front of the body. This latter sign, however, is akin to *maybe, judge,* and relates more to indecision than skepticism. For the present context, the "V" hand in front of the eyes seems to be preferable. It should be noted that the hand may be held some distance from the eyes without loss of clarity or meaning.

Can see For *can* both fists are brought downward to a full stop in front of the body. They may be held so that the palms are downward and the wrists can be bent forward as the sign is executed. *See* is signed by pointing the fingers of the right "V" hand toward the eyes and then bringing the right hand forward from the face. The movement in this case would be toward the imaginary daughter. The line of vision of the signer may also be directed toward the imaginary daughter rather than toward the receiver.

she enjoy If the localization of the daughter has been established effectively, the signer may simply point to that location for the pronominal reference. *Enjoy* is signed by rubbing both palms in a circular motion over the chest and stomach. The right hand is usually placed on the chest and the left on the stomach, but the reverse is often seen. The circular movements are executed simultaneously in opposite directions.

all summer *All* is signed by holding the left hand, palm up, in front of the body, and by bringing the right hand around in a kind of circle, ending with the back of the right hand resting in the palm of the left. The gesture gives an impression of inclusiveness. *Summer* is signed as indicated previously.

Finish say *Finish* is signed as indicated previously, except that it will be linked very closely with *say.* There will be no pause between the two signs.

21

next year This is actually a modulation of the sign for *year*. The circular motion of the right fist around the left is dropped, and the sign begins with the final position, the right fist resting on top of the left. It is then brought forward from the body, adding a temporal marker indicating the *future*. At the same time the numeral *one* is formed by extending the right index finger. The entire gesture is executed as one sign, in which the counter, the temporal marker, and the root of the sign are all embodied in one sequence.

want again go there *Want* draws the "CLAW" hands, palms up, toward the body one or more times. *Again* presents the left hand, palm toward the right and slightly upward, and the right hand is brought up and then downward so that the fingertips of the right hand are placed in the middle of the left palm. Repeated several times in an abbreviated manner the sign means *often. Go there* may be executed as a single gesture, since it should be made in any case off to the right, where the summer camp is localized. Also, if the right index finger is used, the finger will be pointing toward the camp anyway as the sign reaches both its final position and its final configuration. When localization is used as a strategy for indicating absent referents, the direction of movements of some verbs can take such localization into account and the result is a Sign Language narrative with considerable clarity.

We-two stay in Washington two day *We-two* is signed by extending the index and middle finger of the right hand, palm up. The index finger then is directed casually toward the other person or toward the location established for the other person, and the middle finger is moved toward the signer's chest or touched to the chest. The motion may be repeated several times. This is a clear dual, for which English has no equivalent (see Fig. 12).

Stay is signed by thrusting the right "Y" hand forward from the body. The preposition *in* uses the left "O" hand as a point of reference and the fingertips of the right "AND" hand are tucked in the opening of the left "O" hand. *Washington* is signed as

FIG. **12.** *The American Sign Language has a dual,* **we-two,** *for which English has no equivalent.*

indicated previously. *Two day* uses the numeral two on the right hand to mark the sign as plural, and the right forearm moves in an arc representing the sun traversing the sky. Two separate signs are not needed, since the numeral *two* can appear on the right hand as the sign for day is executed.

Me want see there there there people Gallaudet College *Me* and *want* are signed as indicated previously. *See* uses the right "V" hand. The tips of the fingers point toward the eyes, and the right hand is moved forward from the face. *There there there* is a way to indicate that the people who are to be seen are not to be found in one place. It is not a meeting that will be attended, but a number of individual interviews that will be taking place. Since the people are scattered all over the campus, the index finger points to various places around the front of the signer. *Gallaudet College* has a sign that is derived from the name-sign for Gallaudet himself. He wore glasses, and the "G" hand drawn away from the side of the face as if removing glasses is the sign in current use for *Gallaudet College.* The sign for *College* may be added, but it is not really necessary. The sign for *College* is related to the sign for school. In *school* the hands are clapped together as a teacher might clap them together to gain the pupils' attention. *College* strikes the hands together once (in compounds, the first element is often abbreviated) and the right hand then makes a spiral upward circle, indicating a school of "higher" learning.

Daughter want see there there there around Washington *Daughter, want, see* and *there* are signed as indicated previously. *Around* may be a natural gesture which waves the right hand, palm down, in the general region in front of the signer's body. It makes no difference that this same area has just been used to designate various places around the campus of Gallaudet College, since the spatial domain around the signer is his to use as he sees fit and to change as the requirements of the communication warrant. *Washington* is signed as before.

We satisfy limit two day our stay Washington *We* touches the right index finger to the right and to the left shoulder. *Satisfy* is derived from the satisfaction of one's appetite. The two hands, palms down, are placed in a horizontal plane across the chest. Usually the right hand is slightly above the left. They are gently lowered and rested in place as if to imply that the stomach is filled to capacity and the signer is satiated. *Limit* uses bent "B" hands, one above the other, with a twist of the wrist to indicate a span that is not to be exceeded. Only a short distance separates the fingers of the two hands as they are presented so as to represent a *limit. Two day* is signed as indicated previously. *Our* is the first person plural possessive pronoun. It uses the open palm, the general possessive marker, and touches the thumb side of the hand to the right shoulder and then the little finger side of the hand to the left shoulder. The result is an arc formed in

front of the body which has, as its implication, the inclusion of a plural number of persons. *Stay* and *Washington* are signed as indicated previously.

She finish me finish enough The symmetry of this sentence is designed to enhance its effectiveness as a message. The daughter has been localized out front sufficiently frequently that a pointing gesture out to the front is not likely to be mistaken. *Finish* is signed as indicated previously, except that the sign is tied both by the pointing gesture and by the signer's line of vision to the daughter. *Me finish* is executed similarly, except that now the sign for *finish* is attached more closely to the signer's person, perhaps moved closer to his body. *Enough* rubs the right palm over the opening of the left "O" hand. The movement is generally away from the body. Toward the body would be construed without a context as *full*. But either direction is occasionally found for either meaning, with the context serving as the final arbiter.

We-two ready go home *We-two* is signed as indicated previously. *Ready* forms "R" hands with both hands, crosses the wrists, and draws them apart so that the "R" hands point forward, parallel to one another, about waist high. *Go home* is signed as a natural gesture for departing: the right hand is waved off toward the distance. The sign for *home* touches the fingertips of the right "AND" hand to the lips and to the cheek. As an alternative, a sign related to the sign for *leave* can be used, the right "5" hand is drawn off to the side of the head, closing the fingers into the "AND" configuration. This could be literally translated, *Leave* (go) *home*.

VOCABULARY ———————————

1. about (HH-39, TO-110)
2. again (HH-352, TO-191)
3. ago (HH-118, TO-205)
4. airplane (HH-1, TO-651)
5. all (HH-494, TO-193)
6. already (HH-214, TO-174)
7. area (see text)
8. around (HH-433)
9. arrive (HH-221, TO-365)
10. automobile (HH-375, TO-160)
11. autumn (HH-299, TO-283)
12. away (see text)
13. beard (see text)
14. begin (HH-124, TO-458)
15. border (see text)
16. boundary line (see text)
17. but (HH-164, TO-26)
18. camp (fingerspell)
19. can (HH-72, TO-155)
20. car (HH-375, TO-160)
21. close (HH-163, TO-367)
22. college (HH-127, TO-50)
23. congress (HH-107)
24. daughter (HH-500 + 478, TO-275)
25. day (HH-250, TO-182)
26. deaf school (HH-136, TO-417)
27. describe (HH-216, TO-545)
28. doubt (HH-338)
29. drive (HH-375, TO-160)
30. enjoy (HH-42, TO-255)
31. enough (HH-121, TO-534)
32. excited (HH-493, TO-397)
33. experience (HH-373, TO-236)
34. explain (HH-216, TO-545)
35. far (HH-340)
36. far away (HH-340)
37. female (HH-500, TO-106)
38. finish (HH-214, TO-174)
39. first (HH-116, TO-515)
40. fly (HH-1, TO-651)
41. force (HH-355)
42. four (TO-p. 4)
43. fourth (see text)
44. friend (HH-314, TO-638)
45. from (HH-16, TO-33)
46. full (HH-225, TO-538)
47. Gallaudet (HH-463, TO-653)
48. girl (HH-500, TO-106)
49. go (HH-312, TO-114)
50. group (HH-421, TO-412)
51. grow (HH-364, TO-487)
52. hard (HH-367, TO-302)
53. hard work (HH-367, TO-302)
54. her (HH-469)
55. hers (HH-469)
56. his (HH-469)
57. home (HH-489, TO-241)
58. hot (HH-498, TO-136)
59. in (HH-242, TO-14)
60. institution (HH-136, TO-417)
61. interpret (HH-90)
62. its (HH-469)
63. judge (HH-306, TO-559)
64. know (HH-14, TO-206)
65. limit (HH-101, TO-281)
66. live (HH-446, TO-119)
67. male (HH-238, TO-105)
68. man (HH-238, TO-145)
69. maybe (HH-19, TO-51)
70. me (HH-192, TO-2)
71. mine (HH-307, TO-6)
72. my (HH-307, TO-6)
73. near (HH-163, TO-367)
74. never (HH-390, TO-45)
75. next year (HH-497, TO-296)
76. north (HH-161, TO-474)
77. North Carolina (fingerspell N-C)
78. not (HH-249, TO-44)
79. Ohio (fingerspell)
80. old (HH-110, TO-485)
81. on the contrary (HH-164, TO-26)
82. one (TO-p. 4)
83. our (HH-410, TO-7)
84. over (HH-214, TO-174)
85. person (HH-18, TO-426)
86. person marker (HH-18)
87. ready (HH-275, TO-450)
88. ride along (see text)
89. same (see text)

90. satisfy (HH-190, TO-282)
91. say (HH-383, TO-216)
92. second (see text)
93. see (HH-381, TO-207)
94. seventh (see text)
95. she (HH-403)
96. six (TO-p. 4)
97. sixteen (TO-p. 5)
98. south (HH-161, TO-474)
99. South Carolina (fingerspell S-C)
100. spring (HH-364, TO-487)
101. stay (HH-278, TO-647)
102. strict (HH-367)
103. string (see text)
104. study (HH-82, TO-519)
105. summer (HH-441, TO-634)
106. teach (HH-123, TO-253)
107. teacher (HH-123 + 18)
108. ten (TO-p. 4)
109. their (HH-469)
110. theirs (HH-469)

111. there (TO-727)
112. third (see text)
113. thread (see text)
114. three (TO-p. 4)
115. thrilled (HH-493, TO-397)
116. time (HH-187, TO-595)
117. to (HH-240, TO-30)
118. truly (HH-291, TO-219)
119. two (TO-p. 4)
120. two day (see text)
121. United States (fingerspell U.S.)
122. want (HH-448, TO-173)
123. Washington, (TO-443)
124. we two (see text)
125. where (HH-183, TO-28)
126. why (HH-8) TO-16)
127. winter (HH-272, TO-158)
128. work (HH-86, TO-161)
129. world (HH-499, TO-452)
130. year (HH-349, TO-295)
131. your (HH-469, TO-8)

EXERCISES

Sign the following sentences and provide an English translation

1. My friend want go far away N.C.; want stay two day, stay three day.

2. Ago me old sixteen me excited; want see world.

3. Three year ago me want go college. Two year me work. Last fall me go, begin college.

4. You me we two drive Washington see Gallaudet College.

5. Maybe next year summer you me fly south area see area.

6. My friend have daughter three; live near home two, live far away one.

7. Your home where? N.C.? S.C.? where?

8. My teacher old, strict, all time force study.

9. Two year ago me institution finish. Fall ago me begin Gallaudet College.

10. Me know girls three; first go Washington, go Gallaudet College; second go work N.C., third stay home.

Lesson Three

ENGLISH ORIGINAL

A Visit to Mother's New House

Two weeks ago I got a letter from my mother. She wanted me to come see her new house. I couldn't go until yesterday because I was sick. I had to see the doctor every day. The doctor told me to stay home. He said it was all right for me to come to see him, but that I should not go out for any other reason. He said if I didn't listen he would put me in the hospital. I didn't want to get stuck in a hospital for several days, so I did what he said. I stayed home until I was well again. Yesterday was the first time I could go out and do as I pleased. I visited my mother's house for about an hour and a half. Her house is really nice. Last night I was tired when I got home. I loafed all morning.

SIGN LANGUAGE GLOSS

Visit Mother Her New House

Two-weeks+ago get letter from mother. Want me come (pause) see new house. Can't go until yesterday. Why? Sick. Must see doctor every-day. Doctor say, Stay home (pause) Come see me, O-K, other out, No. Not listen (pause) go hospital. Stuck in hospital one, two, three, day don't want. Accept. Stay home until well again. Yesterday first time out free. Visit mother her house about hour half. House truly nice. Yesterday night arrive home tired. All-morning loaf.

Two-weeks + ago The sign for *week* can be executed with the numerals one, two, or three formed on the right hand as the sign is executed to indicate one week, two weeks, or three weeks, respectively. In this case, the left hand is held palm up, and the right "2" hand, palm down, is brushed outward from the body across the up-turned left palm. Then the right "2" hand is thrown backward over the right shoulder to indicate the past tense. The regular past marker is the right hand, palm facing backward, thrown backward over the right shoulder. In this case, the right hand configuration is controlled by the previous sign, *two-weeks*, and the right hand retains the "2" as it is thrown backward over the right shoulder.

get Since the past tense has already been indicated by the past marker attached to *two-weeks*, an additional past tense marker is not required for the verb, *get*. The subject of the sentence, *I*, is understood. The ordinary sign for *get* is executed by bringing both "5" hands toward the chest, ending as fists or "S" hands in the final position (see Fig. 13). But signs are sometimes modified so as to fit the situation (see Fig. 13). In this case, a letter is a small, light object. The sign for *get* may be executed with one hand drawn toward the body and ending as an "A" hand grasping an envelope.

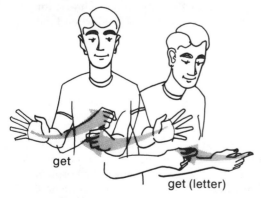

get

get (letter)

FIG. **13.** *The execution of a sign may be modified so as to suit the circumstances.*

letter There is no American Sign Language equivalent for the distinction made in English between definite and indefinite articles. Articles do not appear in American Sign Language. *Letter* is signed by "stamping" the left palm in the upper right hand corner with the right thumb. A longer version touches the right thumb to the lips first, as if licking the stamp before attaching it.

from the curved right index finger is drawn toward the body from the outstretched left index finger. As with many prepositions, the meaning is expressed by the movement of the right hand in relation to the left.

mother The possessive pronoun, *my*, is understood, and it is omitted. American Sign Language often omits modifiers that are implied by the context. The sign for *mother* is the same as the sign for *father* except for the location in which it is executed.

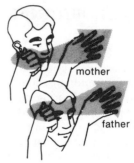

mother

father

FIG. **14.** *The signs for* **father** *and* **mother** *illustrate the role of location as a distinctive feature, as the hand configurations and movements are the same for both.*

Father is signed in front of the forehead, while *mother* is executed in front of the chin, illustrating the role of location as a distinctive feature (see Fig. 14). Both signs begin as "A" hands and end as "5" hands. The movement is off to the left. The two-handed sign is likely to be used only in very formal circumstances. Young children may jab the thumb of the right "5" hand against the chin one or more times, and still younger children, possibly because they lack muscle control, may touch the chin with the index finger of the right "5" hand, a kind of "baby talk" in Sign Language. The forehead and the chin are locations which serve as gender markers in American Sign Language and distinguish the male from the female signs (see Fig. 15). Other examples are male and female *cousin* (right temple vs. right cheek) and *nephew* and *niece* (right temple vs. right cheek). *Cousin*, *nephew* and *niece* are initialized signs.

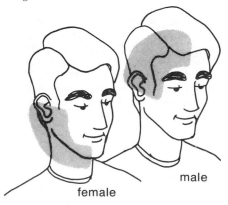

FIG. 15. *The region of the forehand serves as the male gender marker and the region of the right cheek and chin serves as the female gender marker.*

want The curved "5" hands, palms up, are drawn toward the body. This hand configuration may also be referred to as open "C" hands or "CLAW" hands. Both the subject, *She*, and the tense (past) are understood from the context.

me The right index finger is pointed to the chest.

come The index fingers are brought toward the body in an arc. An opposite movement means *go*. This is an infinitive, and English requires the infinitive construction, *to come*. American Sign Language does not have a special grammatical construction to differentiate signs used as infinitives, but the usage and the meaning are the same as in English. It would be permissible here to sign *go* instead of *come* in order to establish the location of the mother's house relative to the person of the signer. Once localized, the position of the house can remain fixed

for the remainder of the message, and all future references to the house can be made by pointing in that direction. Any verbs involving action relative to the house should be executed in the appropriate direction, given the location that has been adopted. In effect, the signer constructs an imaginary stage around himself. Once he has localized objects or people on that stage, he can refer to them by pointing to their location, he can act upon them or have them engage in action by directing the movement of the signs either toward or away from their location, and he can move them about, changing their location relative to each other, as the message unfolds. In this case, the stage is relatively uncluttered: the only important person is the mother, and the only important object is the house. Under these circumstances, localization, while compatible with proper American Sign Language usage, is not required. As the number of people or houses under discussion increases, localization becomes increasingly necessary. But keeping three different houses straight as to what happened where is easier in American Sign Language than in English, since their location relative to the signer makes it possible to reference any of them unambiguously. English would require relative pronouns and descriptive clauses to specify which of the houses was being referenced.

see The conjunction, *and*, although permissible here, is not necessary. A slight pause accomplishes the same effect as the coordinate conjunction. Such a pause allows the receiver to speculate as to why the mother wants the person to come, and the next message supplies the answer, namely, to see her new house. *See* is signed by bringing the right "V" hand forward from eye level.

new house The possessive pronoun, *her*, is omitted. If the result of the omission were to leave some ambiguity as to whether it was the mother's new house or some other new house that the person was to see, this would force the pronoun. The sequence of adjective-noun is not fixed by grammatical rule in American Sign Language. In many instances the sequence is reversed, noun-adjective, as in *house big, car new*. If *new* were an important descriptive adjective, distinguishing the mother's house from other houses, the noun-adjective sequence might be preferred. The sign for *new* grazes the left palm with the back of the right hand moving from right to left in front of the body. *House* is iconic; the sign traces the outline of the roof and walls.

can't Here, too, the subject, *I*, and the past tense, *couldn't*, are understood. Note that American Sign Language is not as redundant as English with respect to indicating the time of the action that is being discussed. In English, verbs must agree with one another as to tense, and every time a verb appears, the receiver is given another indication of the time of the action. In American Sign Language the time is generally established at the outset, and all of the subsequent information is given relative to that time frame. Ordinarily American Sign Language users make sure at the beginning of their communication that this time frame is clearly understood. They are likely to make use of direct eye contact, and they may delay proceeding with the message until the receiver has acknowledged with a nod or some other kind of response that he understands the situation and the context of the message that is to follow. In English, the contractions *can't* and *couldn't* imply two words, *can not* and *could not*. In American Sign Language there is a single gesture for the notion of inability or incompetence, executed by striking the right index finger downward across the extended left index finger, palms facing downward. This same sign in other contexts may mean *Don't do that* or *That is not allowed*.

go If the mother's house has already been localized relative to the person of the signer, this sign should be executed in that direction. If not, the deliberate execution of this sign in a specific direction establishes the location of the house relative to the signer for the rest of the discourse. Future references to the house should be consistent with that location.

until The left index finger is held upright, and the right index finger is brought up

and then over in an arc so as to touch the left fingertip.

yesterday *Yesterday*, like *ago*, includes a movement backward across the time line running down the right side of the head and down the right shoulder. One of the time lines used in American Sign Language to distinguish past from future is the one that runs down the right side of the body. Movements backwards across that line, as in *ago* and *yesterday*, are marked as being in the past by the direction of the movement; movements forward from that line, as in *future* and *tomorrow*, are marked as future by the opposite direction of movement (see Fig. 16). The thumb of the right "A" hand is used to designate *yesterday*. One version moves the thumb backwards along the right cheek; the other touches the thumb to the chin and to the right shoulder.

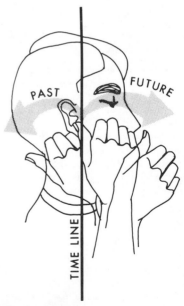

FIG. 16. *Temporal frames of reference are represented by spatial domains extending backward (past) or forward (future) from a time line running down the right side of the body.*

Yesterday and *tomorrow* are executed with the same or at least a similar hand configuration, the "A" and "Y" hand. It is the direction of movement that adds the time marker, making one past and the other future. There are two other important time lines in American Sign Language. One runs down the left palm and is used in *later* and *previously*. The other runs horizontally across the front of the body and is used in *postpone, during,* and *future*.

why? Instead of using a causal clause (because I was sick), American Sign Language often simply poses the obvious question: *Why?* The right hand, palm toward the forehead, is brought forward from the body and ends in a "Y" configuration. The answer to the question is given in the next statement.

sick Here too, the subject, *I*, and the verb, *was*, are understood. *Sick* is signed by touching the middle fingertips of both hands to the forehead and the stomach simultaneously. If only one hand is used, the middle finger of the right hand touches the forehead.

must A downward movement of the curved index finger of the right hand implies varying degrees of compulsion, depending on the forcefulness of the gesture, the body posture, and the accompanying facial expression. In this case, a single sharp jerk downward would probably be sufficient, perhaps with the head cocked slightly at an angle to indicate that the compulsion is aversive. In other contexts a singular gesture may mean simply *should* or *ought*.

see doctor For *see* the right "V" hand is brought forward from the eyes. For *doctor* the right "M" or "D" hand is placed on the pulse area of the left wrist. *Nurse* is signed similarly: the right "N" hand is placed on the pulse area of the left wrist.

every-day These words are hyphenated in the gloss to indicate that a single American Sign Language gesture encompasses both words. The hand configuration of the sign, the "A" hand, is similar to *tomorrow* and *yesterday*. *Tomorrow* moves forward along the cheek; *yesterday* moves backward. *Every-day* is an example of a change meaning as a function of repetition. The sign literally means *tomorrow, tomorrow, tomorrow*. Other examples of this strategy are *week, week, week* for *every week* or *weekly* and *house, house, house* for *city*.

doctor Note the omission of the definite article.

say The past tense is understood. American Sign Language does not require quotation marks, although curved "V" hands may be used to mark off quotes in the air. If it is clear from the context that what follows is a quote, they would probably be omitted unless they were desired for emphasis. Also, American Sign Language does not have a grammatical construction parallel to the English indirect discourse: *The doctor said that I should stay home. Say* is signed by moving the right index finger forward from the lips several times in a small circle.

stay home The imperative is indicated by role playing. The signer assumes a stern facial expression and an authoritative body posture as he forcefully signs *stay home*. For *stay* the right "Y" hand is moved abruptly forward and downward. *Home* is signed by touching the fingertips of the right "AND" hand to the lips and cheek.

Come see me, O-K; other out, no. This, of course, is not a literal translation in American Sign Language of what was said in English. This is a forceful American Sign Language paraphrase, faithful to the intent of the original but departing considerably from the original text. *O-K* is borrowed from English. It is fingerspelled. As it is fingerspelled, the right arm may be drawn backward for the "O" and then moved forward for the "K" with an appropriate tilt of the head. Such a movement accompanying fingerspelling suggests that the fingerspelled symbol is not merely borrowed from English but incorporated into American Sign Language as a special kind of sign. *Other* is signed by moving the right "A" hand, thumb up, off to the right. *Out* draws the right "AND" hand out of the left "C" hand. *No* is an elision of the fingerspelled *N-O:* The middle and index fingers of the right hand are brought down forcefully on the thumb. The hand may be swung downward to add emphasis. The elision of fingerspelled *N-O* into the sign *no* may be a result of a process similar to that observed in *O-K*.

Not listen (pause) go hospital. Again, this is a succinct American Sign Language paraphrase of the conditional clause, *If you do not listen, you will have to go to the hospital*. The condition is clearly implied by the context, and the sign, *If*, is not necessary. The pause helps to establish the notion of a condition: Once the possibility of not listening to the doctor's advice is raised, one can begin to speculate about the possible consequences. The next message satisfies any question that might be raised about such possible consequences. *Not* is signed by bumping the thumb of the right "A" hand under the chin as it moves forward from the body. *Listen* cups the right "C" hand to the right ear.

go hospital This would be signed forcefully with a stern facial expression. The signer is here taking the role of the physician delivering the ultimatum rather than his own role as receiver. Thus, the physician's authority and his seriousness of purpose are portrayed with the facial expression and the body posture of the signer. Such role playing is a frequent phenomenon in American Sign Language usage. The signer may take on multiple roles in any one discourse, changing from one to the other very abruptly, in order to convey not only the gist of the message but also the emotional state of the person who delivered it. It has been pointed out that objects, such as the mother's house, may be localized relative to the person of the signer so that they can be referenced later. The signer constructs an imaginary stage around himself, and he localizes objects and people on that stage so that they can be referenced or so that they can act or be acted upon. Moreover, the signer may occupy the stage himself as he takes the role of one of the persons he is discussing. Skill at dramatization and adroit shifts from one role to another characterize effective strategies of manual communication.

stuck in hospital For *stuck* the right "V" hand is jabbed into the front or side of the neck. This is also a socially restricted sign for *pregnant*. The sign is especially fitting

when the pregnancy is unwanted, but any pregnancy may be indicated the same way. *In* is signed by tucking the fingers of the right "AND" hand into the left "O" hand. As an alternative translation, *Stuck-in* may be indicated by a single sign in which the two fingers of the right "H" hand are jammed into the left "C" hand and held there. The latter version is more forceful.

One, two, three day The explicit indication of *one, two, three day* is a vivid way to depict the notion of *several days*. One literally watches them accumulate before one's eyes. The numerals *one* through *ten* are depicted in Figure 17.

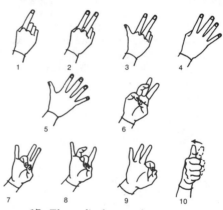

FIG. **17.** *The cardinal numerals one to ten.*

The numerals preceding *day* mark it as a plural. A smoother execution of the same counting sequence might be translated *few* or *several*. *Day* traces the movement of the sun across the sky with the right index finger as the elbow of the right arm rests in the left palm. A lazy imitation of such a complete execution is generally sufficient to be recognized.

don't-want The hyphen in the gloss implies that this is one sign in the American Sign Language lexicon. As a matter of fact, it is a sign with a negation marker attached (see Fig. 18). The sign for *want* draws the curved "5" hands, palms up, toward the body one or more times. In the sign for *don't-want* the curved "5" hands, palms up, are turned over forcefully as if dumping out their contents. Turning the palm away from the body also negates *good*. The sign is executed last in this statement for emphasis: *Stuck in hospital . . . don't want.*

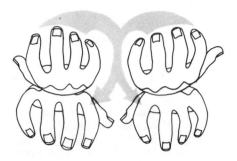

FIG. **18.** *Negation may be indicated by turning the palms of the hands outward and away from the body.*

Accept. This sign is used in a general sense for accepting anything, including a gift. In this context it implies unwilling compliance. It is often signed with one hand, and the lips may be pinched together to indicate distaste at the thought of obeying. The final position of the sign presents the "AND" hand or "AND" hands closed against the chest, fingers pointing downward.

Stay home These are the same signs used previously as the doctor's orders. They would be signed less forcefully, since the signer is now speaking for himself.

Until well again *Until* is signed as described previously. *Well* places the palms on the chest and then brings them forward forcefully, ending as fists or "S" hands. *Again* holds the left palm toward the right, and the right hand is brought up in an arc so that the fingertips of the right hand touch the left palm. Repeated, *again, again, again* means *often*.

Yesterday This is the same sign as was used previously.

first This is the ordinal adjective, and it is ordinarily signed by striking the right index finger against the upraised left thumb. *Second, third,* and *fourth* are indi-

cated by striking the right index finger against the left index finger, middle finger, and little finger, respectively, as the left hand forms the numerals two, three, and four.

time The right index finger touches the left wrist where a watch is likely to be worn.

out free *Out* can be construed as a verb, *go out*, or as a predicate adverb. *Free* is signed by crossing the wrists together as if they were bound and then pulling them apart. The sign may be initialized by forming "F" hands and then executing the sign. As an illustration of the relative freedom of American Sign Language from the kind of order constraints that are typical in English, these four signs, *first time out free*, can be ordered in any of the following sequences:

> (first time out free)
> (first time free out)
> (time first out free)
> (time first free out)

This is not to suggest, however, that there are no order constraints at all in American Sign Language. The following sequences are not permissible:

> (first free out time)
> (time out free first)

The two clusters (first time) and (out free) cannot intrude on each other without implying great changes in the meaning of the message. Of course, the clusters can be interchanged as long as each cluster is kept intact:

> (first time out free)
> (out free first time)

Either of the above is permissible.

Visit mother Visit is signed with the two "V" hands circling outward from the body alternately. The palms are turned toward the face. If the right "V" hand is turned over, palm down, and jumped around in front of the body, the sign means *travel*.

her house The possessive pronoun often follows the noun that it modifies. There are two other manual methods of indicating possession. The "S" hand is sometimes hooked in the air after the noun to suggest an apostrophe-s, and persons using Signed English may move the right "R" hand out from the right cheek to sign *her*. The American Sign Language possessive marker is an open palm. Here it would be directed toward the place where the mother's house has previously been localized.

about The right index finger circles the clustered fingers of the left "AND" hand. To emphasize the approximation involved in estimating how much time was spent in the visit, the signer may shrug or turn his hands, palms up, as if to say, "Oh, about an hour and a half."

hour half *Half* or *one half* is indicated in American Sign Language by signing the numerals *one* and *two* with the *one* placed in space above the *two* (see Fig. 19).

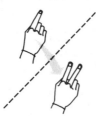

FIG. **19. One-half** *and other fractions are signed by presenting the numerator above the denominator in space in front of the signer.*

Other fractions are signed similarly. For example, *two thirds* is signed by presenting the numeral *two* and then signing *three* underneath it. Compound fractions are represented in the same way that they are printed on a page, that is, the numeral is signed first, and then the fraction is added to the right, the numerator above the denominator. For example, *three and one half*

would be signed by first presenting the numeral, *three*, and then the fraction, *one half*, is signed to the right of the *three*, the *one* above the *two*. *Hour half* in American Sign Language is equivalent to *an hour and a half* in English.

Yesterday night *Ago* + *night* is ambiguous. It could refer to any night in the past. Of course, the context implies that it was *last night*, but the most precise way to translate the English *last night* into American Sign Language is to sign *yesterday night*.

arrive home *Arrive* is signed by holding the left hand, palm up, in front of the body, and the back of the right hand is brought forward and down into the left palm. *Home* touches the tips of the right "AND" hand to the mouth and cheek. This sign is said to refer to *home* as a place where one eats and sleeps.

tired The fingertips of both hands are touched to the chest at the base of the rib cage. The fingers collapse as the hands are rolled downward on the body, as if they are too tired to maintain their position.

All-morning The hyphen implies that this is executed as a single sign in American Sign Language. The right arm is brought all the way up to the noon position as the sign for *morning* is executed, implying that the action occupied the entire morning.

loaf This is a reversal of the sequence that is typical in English. The verb is reserved for last for emphasis. The sign is said to be derived from the posture assumed by a person when he tucks his thumbs under his suspenders as if enjoying a sedentary life. The sign also means *vacation*.

34

VOCABULARY

1. about (HH-39, TO-110)
2. accept (HH-218, TO-331)
3. again (HH-352, TO-191)
4. ago (HH-118, TO-205)
5. all morning (HH-228, TO-183)
6. arrive (HH-221, TO-365)
7. big (HH-473, TO-429)
8. can't (HH-372, TO-39)
9. car (HH-375, TO-160)
10. city (HH-154, TO-351)
11. come (HH-204, TO-113)
12. couldn't (HH-372, TO-39)
13. cousin (HH-220, TO-510)
14. day (HH-250, TO-182)
15. doctor (HH-93, TO-428)
16. don't do that (HH-372, TO-39)
17. don't want (HH-282, TO-173)
18. during (HH-174, TO-102)
19. every day (HH-104, TO-90)
20. father (HH-160, TO-140)
21. few (HH-496, TO-240)
22. first (HH-116, TO-515)
23. fourth (HH-116)
24. free (HH-467, TO-294)
25. from (HH-16, TO-33)
26. future (HH-360, TO-201)
27. get (HH-445, TO-604)
28. go (HH-312, TO-114)
29. go out (HH-242, TO-15)
30. half (see text)
31. her (HH-469)
32. home (HH-489, TO-241)
33. hospital (HH-201, TO-614)
34. hour (HH-422, TO-533)
35. house (HH-154, TO-350)
36. I (HH-70, TO-1)
37. in (HH-242, TO-14)
38. last night (see text)
39. later (HH-262, TO-531)
40. letter (HH-139, TO-511)
41. listen (HH-224, TO-411)
42. loaf (HH-167, TO-425)
43. me (HH-192, TO-2)
44. mother (HH-488, TO-138)
45. must (HH-62, TO-628)
46. my (HH-307, TO-6)
47. nephew (HH-220)
48. new (HH-212, TO-74)
49. nice (HH-112, TO-48)
50. niece (HH-220)
51. night (HH-308, TO-186)
52. no (HH-380, TO-42)
53. not (HH-50, TO-43)
54. nurse (HH-93, TO-428)
55. often (HH-352, TO-192)
56. O-K (fingerspell)
57. one (see text)
58. one half (see text)
59. other (HH-348, TO-91)
60. ought (HH-62, TO-628)
61. out (HH-242, TO-15)
62. past (HH-118, TO-205)
63. postpone (TO-550)
64. pregnant (see text)
65. previously (HH-30, TO-204)
66. say (HH-383, TO-216)
67. second (HH-116)
68. see (HH-381, TO-207)
69. several (HH-496, TO-240)
70. should (HH-62, TO-628)
71. sick (HH-20, TO-387)
72. stay (HH-278, TO-647)
73. stuck (HH-260)
74. that is not allowed (HH-372, TO-39)
75. third (HH-116)
76. three (see text)
77. three and one half (see text)
78. time (HH-187, TO-595)
79. tired (HH-63, TO-278)
80. tomorrow (HH-104, TO-92)
81. travel (TO-603)
82. truly (HH-291, TO-219)
83. two (see text)
84. two thirds (see text)
85. two weeks ago (HH-10)
86. until (HH-145, TO-31)
87. vacation (HH-167, TO-425)
88. visit (HH-227, TO-300)
89. want (HH-448, TO-173)

90. week (HH-326, TO-462)
91. weekly (TO-462)
92. well (HH-382)

93. why? (HH-8, TO-16)
94. yesterday (HH-104, TO-93)

EXERCISES

Sign the following sentences and provide an English translation.

1. Sick, loaf all-day, OK; well, not-allowed.

2. Car my stuck; must go get father.

3. See doctor don't-want; postpone.

4. Me can't come every-day; can't.

5. First day sick, second day see doctor, third day in hospital.

6. Yesterday get letter; say my nephew two will visit.

7. Travel OK; doctor say; can visit you tomorrow.

8. Every-day stuck home, loaf; want go-out, visit.

9. My new car arrive yesterday.

10. Nice letter me get last week from cousin.

Lesson Four

ENGLISH ORIGINAL

The Automobile

It is hard to believe that 50 years ago there were no paved roads, no parking lots, no traffic jams, nothing that had anything to do with cars. Now it is estimated that 20% of our nation's jobs depend directly or indirectly on the automobile. That sounds like an exaggeration until one remembers that auto manufacturers and auto owners are the main support for two basic industries, steel and oil. Add to that all the people who make, sell, repair, or drive cars for a living and you have a small army. Now our great dependence on the automobile is threatening the life of our major cities. It has allowed people to move out to the suburbs, creating urban sprawl. It required paving the downtown with parking lots and cutting up residential areas with freeways. Now it is making the air unfit to breathe. The car has left our cities ugly by day and deserted at night. If only we could go back to the 1920's and start over again, we might have second thoughts about trading our horses for cars.

SIGN LANGUAGE GLOSS

Car

True hard believe (pause) 50 year ago no nice road, road. No many parking-lot there, there, there. No traffic line-up. Nothing connected-with car. Now car true important. Figure, car gone (pause) 20% people, their J-O-B gone. Seem exaggerate? Not. Must remember, (Pause) make car, (pause) need S-T-E-E-L. Want go, travel, car need O-I-L, G-A-S. Car support two big factory, S-T-E-E-L and O-I-L. Add-together people make car, people sell, people fix, people need car for earn money, live (pause) add-together, count, many many people. Now trouble. See we truly need car. Now awful in city. People have car, can move far, scatter, commute work, shop. City spread. Downtown must scrape, scrape, scrape make big park place. People live place, must destroy, make wide-street, wide-street, wide-street. Now make A-I-R lousy, N.G., can't breathe. Car make city ugly during day, bare during night. Wish again 1920, over-again, maybe think. Horse better; keep. Trade for car? No!

GRAMMATICAL NOTES

True The sign, *true,* in which the index finger of the right hand is brought forward from the mouth, is often used to emphasize a statement. It is just as well translated as an adverb, *truly.* Although it occurs in this Gloss as a rough equivalent for "It is," the sign should not be construed as a translation for the English copulative verb, *is, am, are.* Other English equivalents for this sign are *really, actually, as a matter of fact.*

hard The sign for *hard* is related to the sign for *rock.* In *rock* the back of the right fist is struck against the back of the left fist. In *hard* the index and middle fingers of the right hand are bent as the rest of the hand forms a fist. This is sometimes called a bent "V" hand. The knuckle of the middle finger of the right hand is then struck against the back of the left fist. Undoubtedly this sign originally meant *hard* in a physical sense, but by analogy it has come to mean also mentally *hard.* There is another sign for *difficult* which is related to both *hard* and *rock*: the bent "V" hands are moved up and down alternately in front of the body, and the knuckles of the hands are bumped against each other as they pass each other in opposite directions.

believe This is a compound sign, *think* + clasped hands. Presumably the clasped hands suggest that one is holding on to something that is thought and, therefore, believed. This is the sign that translates *believe* in prayers such as The Apostle's Creed: "I believe in God the Father etc."

50 The sign for *50* is formed in much the same way as other numbers that are even multiples of ten. The right hand forms the number "5" and then "0." Sometimes the hand is moved slightly to the right as the "0" is executed. The same procedure is used for *30, 40, 60, 70, 80,* and *90.* The sign for *10* wiggles the upraised thumb of the right hand. The sign for *20* touches the index finger and thumb of the right hand together several times while the other fingers are clenched into a fist.

year The sign for *year* is said to be derived from the revolution of the earth around the sun; the right "S" hand makes a complete circle around the left fist, coming to rest on top of the left fist. A plural marker is not necessary, since the modifier, *50,* plainly indicates the plural.

ago This is the past marker; the right palm is moved backward across the time line on the right side of the head.

no There are a variety of ways to indicate *no, nothing, none* in American Sign Language. One way to indicate a variety of negations is to simply shake the head from side to side in a natural gesture that would also be understood among hearing persons. Here it is appropriate to use the two "O" hands. In their initial position they are placed together in front of the body. They are then moved abruptly apart.

nice The right palm scrapes outward across the upturned left palm. In other contexts the sign may mean *clean.*

road road Sometimes a distinction is made in American Sign Language between *street* and *road; street* is signed with a straight movement forward from the body, while *road* is signed with curving movements forward from the body. But this distinction is somewhat arbitrary and depends on the context. In this case, *road* would probably be signed the same as *street* with no unnecessary movements. It is more important here that the sign be repeated several times to imply a network of *roads* and *highways.* To create such an impression, the sign might be executed in different directions so as to reference all the roads that exist.

no many parking-lot The meaning here is not that there are not many parking lots but that there are none at all. The *no* modifies *parking-lot* rather than *many.* The many parking lots that now exist are zeroed out by the sign *no.* To emphasize the negation, the signer may shake his head from side to side while signing *parking-lot.* The sign for *parking lot* is derived from a general sign for *vehicle* that is commonly used for *ship*: the right hand is held, palm left, with the index and middle fingers extended and the thumb raised up in the air. If this hand configuration is placed on the left palm as the left palm rises and falls as if following the crest of the waves and swells at sea, the sign means *ship*. If the same hand configuration is maneuvered around in the way in which a car is maneuvered as for parallel parking or pulling off the road, it means *car* or some activity associated with using a car. Here, by lining up a number of *cars* in a row on the flat of the left palm, the sign means *parking lot.*

there there there The sign for *parking-lot* is made plural by pointing to several places around the imaginary city (see Fig. 20).

traffic The "5" hands are held, palms facing, and they are moved rapidly past each other in opposite directions so as to represent cars passing each other rapidly. The sign can be shaded in its meaning so as to imply either very rapidly moving *traffic*, as on a freeway, or very congested *traffic*, as on a downtown street.

line-up The "3" hands are placed so that the right hand is behind the left. The right hand is then brought back toward the right shoulder, indicating a long line of items in a row. The same sign can be used for any kind of line-up, such as standing in line for tickets or at a grocery store cash register. The "4" hands or the "5" hands may be used.

nothing To distinguish between *no, none* as used previously and *nothing*, this sign can be executed with a slight variation: the "O" hands can open into "5" hands as the sign is completed. But this is an arbitrary matter, reflecting stylistic reasons for introducing variety into one's signing. It should not be assumed that the parallel usages in American Sign Language have anything to do with the English words. There is an alternate sign for *nothing:* The right "A" hand is placed under the chin and is thrown forward as it opens into a "5" hand.

connected-with This sign is the same as the sign for *join*, except that the hands may be moved forward and backward several times for emphasis.

car Here the common sign for *car* would be used: The hands imitate the motions required for turning a steering wheel. This puts the sign for car in a special category of signs that still retain an idiosyncratic feature derived from the aspect of their referent that they imitate. There is a general tendency in American Sign Language for signs to change over time and to resemble more and more the features of other signs. Movement is one of the features of signs that tends to become stereotyped, so that movements that at one time may have acted out an imitative pantomime are likely to be abbreviated. The sign for *car* has not yet undergone such a transformation: the movement still follows the contour of a steering wheel, and this movement is not used for other conventional signs.

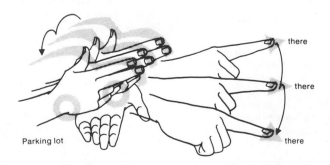

FIG. 20. Parking-lot *is pluralized by pointing to several imaginary locations.*

Now The bent "B" hands are brought down to a full stop at the imaginary line which provides a time marker in front of the body.

true This sign merely adds emphasis to the term following.

important The "F" hands, palms facing, are brought up in front of the body and then together so that the tips of the thumb and index fingers of both hands touch. An alternate version twists the wrists as the hands are raised so that the circles formed by both "F" hands are placed against each other. Differences such as these in the manner of executing a sign are often a result of regional dialects. The sign also means *worth, worthy, valuable.* The same hand configuration is also used for the signs *judge* (the "F" hands move up and down alternately in front of the body) *decide* (*think* is followed by both "F" hands brought forcefully down to a full stop in front of the body) and *condemn* (the right "F" hand strikes the thumb and index finger of the left "F" hand as the right hand is brought forcefully downward). It is an interesting feature of American Sign Language that groups of signs which share semantic properties may also share a structural feature. In this case, all the signs are evaluative, and they all use the "F" hand configuration. Signs involving mental activity are signed at or near the forehead. Signs involving feeling or emotion use the middle finger of one or both hands. Signs involving the future move forward; signs involving the past move backward. Thus, the location, the hand configuration or the movement can serve as a common feature of signs that share some aspect of their meaning.

Figure This sign is the same as is used for *multiply,* but it is executed in a smaller space and with a facial expression that implies mental concentration. Both "V" hands are held, palms up, in front of the body, and the hands are brought together so that the right hand crosses repeatedly over the left.

car gone The effectiveness of this conditional clause is enhanced by the fact that both signs, *car* and *gone* are executed in the same location. Executing the sign for *car* (or fingerspelling *C-A-R*) in front of the body temporarily localizes it there in space. Signing *gone* immediately afterward portrays the disappearance of the car quite dramatically. The sign for *gone* holds the left "C" hand in front of the body, and the right "5" hand is drawn forcefully downward through it as the left hand closes to the "O" hand and the right hand closes to the "AND" hand. The same sign is also used for *disappear, drop out of sight.*

20% The sign for *20* is made by touching the tips of the thumb and index finger of the right hand together several times. *Percent* is executed by tracing a percent sign in the air in front of the body with the right "O" hand, as in Fig. 21. Generally, just the first circle and the slash are executed; the final circle in the lower right is omitted.

FIG. 21. *The sign for* **percent** *traces the major portion of the symbol in the air with the right "O" hand.*

people The "P" hands are moved alternately up and down in front of the body or in a slightly circular motion toward the body. If the two "P" hands are drawn downward once, the sign is singular, *person.* The repeated movement of the "P" hands bobbing up and down alternately implies the plural, *people.*

their This is the possessive marker; the open palm is turned outward to where the people are imagined to be. They have been localized temporarily in front of the body because that is where the sign for *people* has just been executed.

J-O-B It is likely that this word will be fingerspelled. There are a number of English words that are so well known to deaf people that they are likely to have been taken over into their manual system of communication intact through fingerspelling. Lacking a need for a sign equivalent, the English word will continue to serve as a manual label. For similar reasons there are no signs for the makes of cars, the brand names of merchandise, the months of the year, and a number of other things for which English labels are readily available. It would be inappropriate to judge the American Sign Language a deficient language because it lacks sign equivalents for these kinds of referents. The availability of English labels has made it unnecessary for the deaf linguistic community to invent signs for the same referents. Since deaf children ordinarily acquire English and American Sign Language concurrently, they are likely to draw on both languages as they construct a functional system of communication. Whether their labels are derived from English or from American Sign Language is determined by convenience or social convention rather than by real or imagined characteristics of the languages from which their symbols are derived. Moreover, some fingerspelled terms have assumed a status that is more akin to signs than to simple fingerspelling. For example, as J-O-B is fingerspelled, the wrist may be twisted so that the final position shows the palm of the "B" hand turned toward the face of the signer. When fingerspelling is modulated with a movement, it is no longer appropriate to describe the result as a word borrowed from English. The modulation justifies treating the result as an integral feature of American Sign Language.

gone The repetitious use of *gone* for both the jobs and the cars is for the purpose of emphasis. The second time it can be signed somewhat more forcefully, and the body stance of the signer can be held expectantly as if waiting for the point to register fully.

Seem The palm of the right hand, cupped slightly, is gradually turned toward the face as if to allow a glimpse of what is there. The same sign executed alternately with the left and the right hands means *compare*. For *seem* the muscles of the right arm may be tensed as if to convey a feeling of intense interest.

exaggerate The left fist is held near the mouth, and the right fist, originating from the left is brought forward from the body, originating from the left fist, in a waving motion. The sign is related to the sign for *advertise*, which simply strikes the right fist against the left several times as the left fist is held in front of the mouth.

Not This sign is executed somewhat belligerently, as if refuting the earlier suggestion that this is just an exaggeration. The thumb of the right "A" hand is bumped up against the underside of the chin as the hand is moved forward from the body.

Must remember The sign for *must* is the same as has been used previously for compulsion: the right "X" hand is brought downward in front of the body with the force and speed indicating the degree of compulsion. Here a slight movement downward is sufficient. *Remember* gets relatively more emphasis. The sign is a compound, *think + remain*. The right index finger or the right thumb is touched to the forehead, and then the sign for *stay, remain* is executed. Here the sign for *stay* might be repeated several times, suggesting that this may require some ongoing mental effort on the part of the receiver to *remember* or *recall* what is needed for the argument to proceed. Also, the right thumb might be pressed rather forcefully against the left thumb nail, suggesting that the sender is out to make an impression on the other person's memory, having him *recall* certain specific items of information. The facial expression may supplement the effect by showing an air of authority or conviction. There is another sign for *recall* which has a different connotation: the right "5" hand is brought forward from behind the right shoulder up to the front of the face. The sign suggests bringing something back from the past to the present.

make The fists are bumped together as the "S" hands are twisted back and forth, the right hand on top of the left in front of the body. For clarity, the text could reference the *factory* or the *many factory* where cars are made.

need This is the same sign as is used for *must*. It is an unnecessary concession to English to sign *must have*.

S-T-E-E-L Since there is no sign for *oil*, *oil* will have to be fingerspelled. One may as well fingerspell *steel*, as well, for the sake of symmetry.

Want go, travel *Want* is signed by drawing both "CLAW" hands, palms up, toward the body. *Go* moves both index fingers, one pointing down and the other pointing up, in circles around each other as they are moved around in front of the body. An alternative sign holds the bent "V" hand, palm down, and moves the hand around, gesturing downward with the fingertips repeatedly, as if making several stops on a tour.

need O-I-L G-A-S Both *oil* and *gas* are likely to be fingerspelled. One could imitate the filling of a gas tank at a filling station to represent *gasoline*, but that would not solve the problem of a sign for *oil*. As long as one of the terms is fingerspelled, the other may as well be also.

Car support *Car* may be either signed or fingerspelled. *Support* is signed by placing the right fist under the left and raising them both up in front of the body. The backs of the fingers of the right hand are in contact with the little finger edge of the left fist. The sign is related to the sign for *help*, in which the left fist in the same orientation is raised upward by the fingertips of the right palm.

two big factory The sign for *big* is generally executed with the index fingers hooked slightly as if for emphasis. Or the "L" hands can begin back to back and twist outward. The sign resembles the signs *much* (executed with the open palms), *large* ("L" hands), and *very* ("V" hands). *Factory* is derived from the meshing of gears. The bent "5" hands are meshed together in

front of the body as they are turned toward each other one or more times. The same sign also means any kind of *machine* or *machinery*. There is no sign in American Sign Language for *industry* in a generic sense. The two big industries that are supported by the automobile are named again for clarity: *S-T-E-E-L* and *O-I-L*. They may be fingerspelled with opposite hands for rhetorical effect.

Add-together The two "5" hands are brought together vertically in front of the body. As they come together the hands form the "AND" configuration, and in the final position the fingertips are touching. The sign for *with* may be added after the hands are brought together. *With* is signed by placing the clenched fists side by side in front of the body.

people make car Subordinate clauses (people who make cars) are rarely found in American Sign Language. There is a very effective strategy for conveying the notion of subordination: the information that would appear in a dependent clause in English is signed lower down in front of the body and in a smaller amount of space, as in Fig. 22. Then, when the main thought is resumed, the hands resume their former position in front of the body.

FIG. 22. *Subordination may be indicated in American Sign Language by executing the subordinate clause at a lower level and in a smaller space than the main clause.*

Here a string of clauses is planned. One way to arrange these appropriately in American Sign Language is to sign the first one off to the left a bit, the second one slightly to the right *(people sell)*, the third one still farther to the right *(people fix)* and then, finally, the last one farther off to the right *(people need car)*. By arranging the clauses in such a sequence, the syntax itself is ordered appropriately, and the people are neatly localized so that they can be summed together and counted at the end so as to make the point that they constitute a large number of people taken together. The facial expression may mark the verbs (make, sell, fix, and need) with a special cue to indicate that they are in some way related. Raised eyebrows, a slight nod, pinched lips, or a slight forward bending of the upper body may function as such a marker. If the same marker is attached to each verb, this serves to organize them together within the sentence.

people sell The sign for *sell* is said to be derived from the actions of a store clerk holding up a garment and shaking it out so that a potential buyer can see it. The same sign is also used for the noun, *store*. This sign is also used for *sell* in the sense of *peddling*, an activity that is frowned on by the deaf community generally. Occasionally it happens that a person who seems to be deaf will sell pencils or alphabet cards from door to door or in stores and shopping centers. On the one hand, deaf people can be somewhat sympathetic toward a deaf person who resorts to such a tactic on rare occasions when he is in real financial need. But when such activities are organized on a national scale, or when a hearing person impersonates a deaf person and sells such materials, the result is deplored. It gives the general public the impression that deaf people cannot support themselves with gainful employment. The fact is that deaf people have a very good record of employability and job stability. Since the sign *sell* has this possibly negative connotation, one must be careful how it is used.

people fix The sign for *fix* is similar to the sign for *make*. With *fix* there is less twist of the wrists. Many deaf people would probably fingerspell *F-I-X*.

for This is the sign for purpose. It translates the French *pour*.

earn money These two signs are executed almost as a single gesture. For *earn* the right "C" hand is scraped toward the body across the left palm, and for money the back of the right "AND" hand is tapped into the left palm. Once the money is scraped together *(earned)* it is in the palm.

live The same body stance and a facial expression are maintained for *live* as for *earn money*. This continuity of body cues maintains the connection between earning money and living so that they are taken together.

add-together The four clauses that were placed from left to right in front of the body are now swept together with the sign *add-together*. In contrast to the previous, vertical execution of *add-together*, the two "5" hands are brought together from the sides, ending as "AND" hands touching at the fingertips in front of the body.

count Now that the people are all added together, they can be counted up. The right "F" hand touches the left palm in an ascending motion as if totaling up a column.

many many people After the adding and counting are completed, the results are announced. The sequence of signs in this statement may have a bearing on the question of order constraints in American Sign Language. Sign Languages typically follow what has been called "narrative order." There is a certain order associated with actions and events that cannot be ignored. To the extent that American Sign Language recapitulates a series of occurrences, it will follow the sequence in which they took place. In this case, it is appropriate that the people be gathered together before they are counted, and that they be counted before the results are announced.

Now trouble The sign for *trouble* is similar to the sign for *worry*: In *worry* the hands, palms facing, are moved back and forth in front of the face alternately as if brushing cobwebs aside or as if trying to see through a dense fog. In *trouble* the "B" hands, palms facing, are bent simultaneously toward each other once or several times in front of the face. The signer may nod his head for emphasis at the same time he signs *trouble*.

See *See* can be used in American Sign Language in much the same way as it can be used in English to mean *understand*. The sign here would be executed forcefully in order to support the argument.

we The first person plural pronouns *(we, our, us)* touch the right and the left shoulders. The arc that the hand makes as it moves from one shoulder to the other encompasses the group that includes the signer. *We* is signed with the index finger, *our* with the open palm for the possessive, and *us* with the "U" hand, an initialized sign from the English.

truly This sign is inserted for emphasis. It should be executed forcefully with a stern facial expression.

need This is the same sign as *must*.

Now awful The sign for *awful, terrible* uses either "A" hands, "F" hands or "8" hands. They are flicked out to "5" hands as they are thrown up from the head or out from the body.

in The right "AND" hand is tucked into the left "C" or "O" hand.

city The fingertips of the hands are touched together as the hands are moved from left to right across the front of the body. The sign literally means *house, house, house*. Repetition here goes beyond merely pluralizing the noun, since the meaning is essentially different from *houses*. Similar changes in meaning from repetition occur with the signs *tomorrow (daily)* and *week (weekly)*.

People have car For *have* the fingertips of the two hands are touched to the chest of the signer.

can The fists are brought down forcefully in front of the body.

move The "5" hands close into "AND" hands in front of the body and then "move" what they have grasped to another place. This sign is generally restricted to *move* in the sense of changing one's place of residence.

far The "A" hands, thumbs up, are held near each other in front of the body. The right hand is then stretched off to the right a *far* distance from the left. As with prepositions, the left hand provides a point of reference, and the meaning is conveyed by the relation of the right hand to the left. The sign *far* might be repeated several times in different directions to suggest that people are now able to move off in all directions from the central city.

scatter Both "5" hands, palms down, are moved out from the body in an arc as the fingers flutter to represent the people streaming from the city as they move out.

commute The right "A" hand, thumb up, is moved back and forth as if traversing the distance from home to work and back again repeatedly.

work If the previous context has suggested in any way that the city has been localized relative to the signer, the signs for *work* and *shop* should be executed where the city is or in that general direction.

shop The right "AND" hand is brought forward from the left palm as if placing money on a counter one or more times. The sign is related to the sign for *money*. As an alternative, one might sign *sell* for *shop*. After *work* and *shop* have been signed, the sign for *commute* may be repeated.

City spread The "AND" hands are held near the chest, and then both hands move forward from the body as they change to "5" hands. For emphasis, the cheeks may be puffed out with air with the lips pinched together to imply that the city is bulging at the seams from spreading out so far.

Downtown The sign for *downtown* is the same as the sign for *city*; the context has to help to distinguish them. In this case, the sign for *downtown* can be executed more or less in one place, unlike *city*, which was signed by moving the hands across the front of the body as they touched at the fingertips.

Must scrape, scrape, scrape The right hand is bent to form the blade of a bulldozer. The little finger edge of the bent "B" hand is scraped outward along the left palm several times as if moving the dirt aside for construction work.

make big park place The sign for *big* draws the two hands, palms facing, apart from each other in front of the body. For emphasis, the bent "L" hands can be used. The sign for *park* is the same as the sign used previously for *parking lot.* In fact, the sign for *place* does not need to be added here if the sign for *parking lot* is spread over enough area to suggest that it requires a lot of room.

People live place To indicate a residential area of a city, one might indicate that the area is where people live. *People live place* is adequate.

must destroy The sign for *destroy* begins with both hands clenched into fists ("A" hands), and they are scraped together as the right hand is brought forcefully across the knuckles of the left fist as it is moved toward the body. Then, as the right hand is brought out from the body, the palm of the right "5" hand is scraped across the palm of the left hand as if the previous action has flattened everything.

make wide-street The sign for *wide-street* is the same as the sign for *road* used previously, except that the width of the *street* is exaggerated so as to lend force to the argument that a lot of residential housing is being destroyed. For *wide* the palms of the hands may first be touched together before bringing them wide apart so as to add emphasis to the adjective. The sign may be repeated to imply a network of freeways.

Now make A-I-R lousy The sign for *lousy* is mildly socially restricted. It is signed by touching the thumb of the right "3" hand to the nose and then throwing the sign outward and downward from the face. The nose is the location for several signs that are socially restricted. *A-I-R* is fingerspelled.

N-G The fingerspelled *N-G* (for "No Good") has become a common expression in American Sign Language in spite of its obvious derivation from English. When it is

executed, it looks more like a sign than a pair of spelled letters, since the movement from "N" to "G" involves a twist of the wrist. If the two-hand alphabet is used instead of the one-hand alphabet, the movement is even more apparent, since the right hand is struck against the left twice in the two-hand execution of *N G.*

can't breathe A single sign conveys the meaning of *inability.* The right index finger is struck in a downward movement against the left index finger. *Breathe* imitates the movement of the chest when air is inhaled and exhaled: The hands are held near the chest, palms facing the chest, and they are moved forward and back again following the movement of the chest when breathing.

Car make city ugly during day The sign for *ugly* is derived from facial disfigurement. The sign for *during* is not really necessary; *day* can be signed so as to represent the sun moving across the entire horizon so as to imply that the state that is being described here is one that persists throughout the day. The sign for *during* is related to the sign for *happen. Happen* is signed by turning the "G" hands over in front of the body. For *during* a time marker is added; the hands move forward from the body so as to imply a continuation of the action. The sign also translates the English *while.*

bare during night The sign for *bare* is interesting for its versatility. It uses the middle finger of the right hand, suggesting that this sign belongs to a class of signs which suggest feeling or emotion. Others are *touch, feel, pity,* and *sick.* For *bare* the tip of the middle finger of the right hand is stroked outward across the back of the left hand or fist. The sign also means *naked,* and this may be its original meaning, since it literally suggests feeling *bare* skin. But by analogy it has come to mean also a *vacant* house, a *blank* page, an *empty* bucket, and here, *deserted* streets. *Night* also can be signed in such a way as to imply the duration of the night, but the sign for *during* may be used here as a way to call attention to the duration of the time that the city has been affected by the automobile.

Wish The sign for *wish, long for,* is derived from the sign for *hungry.* The right "C" hand draws a "hollow tube" down the chest.

again The left hand is held, palm up, in front of the body, and the fingertips of the right "B" hand are brought up in an arc and then down into the middle of the left palm. Here the sign may be executed somewhat more emphatically than normally, to show strong feeling. The arc may be formed somewhat higher, and the hand may strike the left palm more forcefully.

1920 The years are signed in American Sign Language the same way they are spoken in English: first the *19* and then the *20.* The numerals 11 through 19 are signed with one hand. For *11, 12, 13, 14,* and *15,* the hand is held in front of the body, palm turned slightly upward. For *11* the index finger is flicked out, and for *12* the index and middle fingers are flicked out. For *13, 14,* and *15,* the fingers which form the numerals *3, 4,* and *5,* respectively, are wiggled as the hand is held in the palm up position. For *16* through *19,* the numeral *10* is formed first: The right fist is held with the thumb pointing upward. Then the appropriate numeral is formed. Thus, *10 6* is *16, 10 7* is *17, 10 8* is *18,* and *10 9* is *19.* The year, *1920* is indicated by signing *19* and then *20.*

over-again Both hands are brought forward from the body in a gesture which ends with the palms up in front of the body. The sign resembles a natural gesture meaning something like "There." Eye contact with the palms of the hands may help to establish the meaning, "Let's do it over again." As an alternative, one might repeat the sign for *again* as the eyes stare off in the distance as if imagining the past over again.

maybe Both hands are held, palms up, in front of the body, and they are moved indecisively up and down in front of the body.

think The right index finger is jabbed forcefully toward the forehead as if to imply that this is a new and surprising notion.

horse The right "U" hand is placed against the forehead and wagged forward in imitation of the movement of a horse's ears. Other animals are signed with similar imitations: *mule* with the "B" hand, *cow* with the "Y" hand showing the horn, and *deer* with the "5" hand showing the antlers.

better The fingertips of the right palm are touched to the lips, and the right hand, thumb up, is then raised upward near the side of the face.

keep The right "K" hand is tapped on top of the left "K" hand once with an emphatic downward movement or several times with light taps. It is a general rule in American Sign Language that the amount of movement present in a sign must be plainly visible. Alternate forms of the same sign, therefore, may either use one large movement or several smaller ones. When the movement is shortened, the repetition helps to make up for the reduction in distance traversed by the hand or hands.

trade This is the same sign as would be used for the preposition, *instead of.* The "F" hands are placed in front of the body with the one hand slightly ahead of other. They then exchange places, the one hand moving forward and the other moving toward the body.

for The right index finger is brought forward from the forehead.

car Following the sign for *car,* the hands are held in position and a questioning facial expression indicate that this constitutes a question. "Should we trade our horse for a car?" *C-A-R* may be fingerspelled here and elsewhere in the text. In fact, the fingerspelled execution of *C-A-R* may be as much a part of American Sign Language as *J-O-B.*

No This sign may have evolved from the fingerspelled *N-O.* The right index and middle fingers are brought down forcefully in contact with the right thumb. The right hand may be moved outward and downward vigorously to add emphasis to the answer. If *C-A-R* had been fingerspelled, the left hand may execute *No* directly at the right hand, which has just fingerspelled *C-A-R*, as shown in Fig. 23. Such use of the location in which a sign has been executed, orienting the next sign in that direction so as to relate them, constitutes an important source of structure in American Sign Language. Lexical items that would be related in English by means of word order may be related in American Sign Language by means of their spatial relations over against each other as they are executed.

FIG. **23.** *The spatial arrangement of signs within a sentence may relate signs to each other, thus providing an important source of syntactic structure for American Sign Language.*

VOCABULARY

1. actually (HH-291, TO-219)
2. add together (see text)
3. advertise (HH-153, TO-299)
4. again (HH-352, TO-191)
5. ago (HH-118, TO-205)
6. air (fingerspell)
7. and (HH-46, TO-239)
8. as a matter of fact (HH-291, TO-219)
9. awful (HH-296, TO-548)
10. bare (HH-294, TO-607)
11. believe (HH-203, TO-475)
12. better (HH-342, TO-505)
13. big (HH-473, TO-429)
14. blank (HH-294, TO-607)
15. breathe (see text)
16. can (HH-72, TO-155)
17. can't (HH-372, TO-39)
18. car (HH-375, TO-160)
19. city (HH-154, TO-351)
20. clean (HH-112, TO-48)
21. commute (see text)
22. compare (HH-363, TO-198)
23. connected with (HH-33, TO-543)
24. count (HH-461, TO-495)
25. cow (HH-219)
26. daily (HH-104, TO-90)
27. day (HH-250, TO-182)
28. decide (HH-147, TO-558)
29. deer (HH-219)
30. deserted (HH-294, TO-607)
31. destroy (TO-334)
32. difficult (HH-426, TO-303)
33. disappear (see text)
34. downtown (HH-154, TO-351)
35. during (HH-174, TO-102)
36. earn (HH-447, TO-491)
37. eighteen (TO- p.5)
38. eighty (TO- p.5)
39. eleven (TO- p.4)
40. empty (HH-294, TO-607)
41. exaggerate (HH-153, TO-299)
42. factory (HH-105, TO-248)
43. far (HH-340)
44. feel (HH-442, TO-388)
45. fifteen (TO- p.4)
46. fifty (TO- p.5)
47. figure (HH-132, TO-301)
48. fix (see text)
49. for (HH-404, TO-18)
50. forty (TO- p.5)
51. fourteen (TO- p.4)
52. gas (fingerspell)
53. gone (see text)
54. have (HH-292, TO-268)
55. help (HH-495, TO-526)
56. highway (HH-412, TO-344)
57. horse (HH-219)
58. house (HH-154, TO-350)
59. hungry (HH-165, TO-404)
60. important (HH-343, TO-542)
61. in (HH-242, TO-14)
62. instead of (HH-117, TO-549)
63. job (fingerspell)
64. join (HH-33, TO-543)
65. judge (HH-306, TO-559)
66. keep (HH-304, TO-309)
67. large (HH-473, TO-429)
68. line up (see text)
69. live (HH-446, TO-119)
70. long for (HH-165, TO-404)
71. lousy (HH-398)
72. machine (HH-105, TO-248)
73. machinery (HH-105, TO-248)
74. make (HH-210, TO-298)
75. many (HH-34, TO-657)
76. maybe (HH-19, TO-51)
77. money (HH-447, TO-63)
78. move (HH-286, TO-252)
79. much (HH-473, TO-167)
80. mule (HH-77)
81. multiply (HH-132, TO-301)
82. must (HH-62, TO-628)
83. naked (HH-294, TO-607)
84. need (HH-62, TO-628)
85. nice (HH-112, TO-48)
86. night (HH-308, TO-187)
87. nineteen twenty (TO- p.5)
88. nineteen (TO- p.5)
89. ninety (TO- p.5)

90. no (HH-380, TO-42)
91. no (HH-392, TO-41)
92. no good (fingerspell: N-G)
93. none (HH-392, TO-41)
94. not (HH-249, TO-44)
95. nothing (HH-392, TO-40)
96. now (HH-2, TO-47)
97. oil (fingerspell)
98. our (HH-410, TO-7)
99. over again (see text)
100. park (see text)
101. parking lot (see text)
102. peddle (HH-78)
103. people (HH-320, TO-427)
104. percent (see text)
105. person (HH-18, TO-426)
106. pity (HH-148, TO-389)
107. place (HH-44, TO-433)
108. really (HH-291, TO-219)
109. recall (see text)
110. remain (HH-278, TO-647)
111. remember (HH-226 + 278, TO-118)
112. road (HH-143, TO-343)
113. rock (HH-232)
114. scatter (see text)
115. scrape (see text)
116. see (HH-381, TO-207)
117. seem (HH-363, TO-203)
118. sell (HH-78, TO-242)
119. seventeen (TO- p.5)
120. seventy (TO- p.5)
121. ship (HH-231)
122. shop (TO-66)
123. sick (HH-20, TO-387)
124. sixteen (TO- p.5)
125. sixty (TO- p.5)
126. spread (HH-245)
127. steel (see text)

128. store (HH-78, TO-242)
129. street (HH-412, TO-344)
130. support (HH-495, TO-527)
131. ten (TO- p.4)
132. terrible (HH-296, TO-548)
133. their (HH-469)
134. there (see text)
135. think (HH-226, TO-79)
136. thirteen (TO- p.4)
137. thirty (TO- p.5)
138. tomorrow (HH-104, TO-92)
139. touch (HH-458, TO-590)
140. trade (HH-117, TO-131)
141. traffic (see text)
142. travel (TO-603)
143. trouble (HH-357, TO-380)
144. true (HH-291, TO-219)
145. truly (HH-291, TO-219)
146. twelve (TO- p.4)
147. twenty (TO- p.5)
148. two (TO-p.4)
149. ugly (HH-171, TO-633)
150. us (HH-432, TO-5)
151. vacant (HH-294, TO-607)
152. valuable (HH-343, TO-542)
153. vehicle (see text)
154. very (HH-473, TO-313)
155. want (HH-448, TO-173)
156. we (HH-137, TO-4)
157. week (HH-326, TO-462)
158. weekly (TO-462)
159. wide street (see text)
160. wish (HH-165, TO-404)
161. with (HH-476, TO-20)
162. work (HH-86, TO-161)
163. worry (HH-357, TO-380)
164. worth (HH-343, TO-542)
165. worthy (HH-343, TO-542)
166. year (HH-349, TO-295)

EXERCISES

Sign the following sentences and provide an English translation.

1. Factory big; many people work; must have parking-lot big.

2. Keep car, trade car, must decide; hard.

3. Year+ago+two buy horse; money how-much can't remember.

4. Night ago think car trouble; pull-over, look G-A-S gone, bare.

5. Ago think must have house big, car nice; now seem not important.

6. Want money much? Can. Must save weekly, save, save, save, add-together: much.

7. Week+ago sick; feel lousy; now feel fine; can drive downtown, shop.

8. Many year ago live far, commute-far; move, commute-short; save money.

9. Week+ago car line-up far, can't understand; look, big rock in street.

10. Mule work hard, can; worth money much.

Lesson Five

ENGLISH ORIGINAL

Washington, D.C., My Second Home

I have been to Washington, D.C., many times, but I never pass up a chance to go back for another visit. I especially enjoy Washington in the Spring when the cherry blossoms are in full bloom and all of the other flowering trees and shrubs show their colors. There is no doubt about it. Washington is a beautiful city. Some people complain that the government buildings look like fake Greek temples and that the streets are not safe for people to go out at night. There may be some truth to both of these statements, but not enough to kill my enthusiasm. Of course, I have many friends in Washington, and that makes a big difference. If they all moved to Chicago, maybe I would come to like Chicago. But that is not likely to happen, and I will continue to think of Washington, D.C., as a very special place where I will always feel at home.

SIGN LANGUAGE GLOSS

Washington, D.C., My Second Home

Finish touch Washington, D.C., many time. Nevertheless, can go again visit, never say-no. Washington enjoy best in Spring time. You know C-H-E-R-R-Y B-L-O-S-S-O-M-S. Tree flower, other flower, all-over true beautiful color. Make sure (pause) Washington beautiful place. Some people complain government building all seem false Greek temple, complain go-out street, street night not safe. Maybe true, but me still like. All-right, have friend many in Washington, help much. Judge friend all move Chicago, maybe me change, like Chicago. But seem not happen. Me still think Washington, D.C., nice place. Me always feel same home.

51

GRAMMATICAL NOTES

Finish touch Washington, D.C. This is a common idiomatic expression in American Sign Language. *Finish touch* is equivalent to *I have been to, I have visited.* In answer to the question, "Have you ever been to California?" one might answer, *Finish touch.* In this case the Name-Sign, *Washington, D.C.,* is given as the place previously visited. Many places have Name-Signs as labels. Cities with special Name-Signs that are well-known among deaf people are *New York, Chicago, Philadelphia, New Orleans, Pittsburgh,* and *Detroit. New York* is the right "Y" scraped across the left palm. *Chicago, Philadelphia,* and *Detroit* are initialized signs or abbreviations of fingerspelling: The first letter of the cities is presented forward from the right shoulder and then brought downward in a waving motion. *New Orleans* circles the right "O" hand on the left palm. *Pittsburgh* tucks the thumb and fingertips of the right "F" hand in an imaginary lapel pocket on the left shoulder. There are conflicting anecdotes accounting for the origin of the sign for *Pittsburgh.* Both claim the sign is based on a *Pittsburgh* delegate to a conference. The one story claims he had a cold and was always reaching for a handkerchief. The other story claims he had a pocket full of cigars and was constantly pulling one out. Both stories agree that the sign imitates a mannerism or characteristic behavior of a person from Pittsburgh. Whether either of these stories is true is hard to tell. They are cited here to illustrate one way in which Name-Signs originate. Another way is through association: *California* is based on the sign for *gold. America* represents a split rail fence. Name-Signs for people may also reflect considerable ingenuity, although most of them are initialized from the person's given name. In addition to the nationally known Name-Signs for the cities listed above, deaf people will generally have a Name-Sign for the city in which they live, even if it happens to be a small one. The Name-Sign for *Washington, D.C.,* touches the right "W" to the top of the right shoulder and then makes a small spiral as it is raised in the air off the shoulder.

many time For *many* one or both "A" hands are flicked out to "5" hands one or more times. For *time* the right index finger is touched to the left wrist where a watch is likely to be worn. The sign, *many,* has already pluralized *time;* an additional marker is not needed.

Nevertheless The left bent "B" hand is held with the fingers pointing upward, palm up, and the fingers of the right hand bat the fingers of the left hand back and forth. The sign implies *indifference.* It also translates the English, *anyway.* A more casual execution holds the left hand so that the fingers point toward the right, and they are slapped back and forth by the right hand: *it makes no difference.* In the present context it serves as an adversative conjunction as well, covering the implications of *but* in the English original.

can go again This clause implies a condition: *If I have a chance to go again.* Go is a sign whose antonym is indicated by reversing the movement executing the sign. If the right index finger or both index fingers move forward from the body, the sign means *go;* if they are moved toward the body, the sign means *come. Again* is an example of a sign whose meaning changes somewhat if the sign is repeated. *Again, again, again* means *often.*

visit The "V" hands make circles alternately out from the body. If the body is oriented in various directions as the sign is executed, it means *visit* in the sense of *touring the countryside.*

never This sign may be related to the sign for *no, don't.* In *don't* the hands are held, palms out, with the wrists crossed in front of the body. They are then brought apart emphatically. The head may be turned aside as the sign is executed. *Never* may be a repetition of the sign *no, don't* executed with one hand. The right hand traces a path in front of the body which vaguely resembles the contour of the numeral "2." The two movements off to the right may reflect the *no, no* prohibition that is implied by *never*.

say-no Both hands execute an abbreviated fingerspelling of N-O: the index and middle fingers of both hands are brought down sharply against the thumbs as the hands are moved downward abruptly in front of the body. The sign literally means to say "No" to someone. It can be turned toward the signer to indicate that someone said, "No" to the signer. As an alternative, one might sign *Never refuse, refuse* being signed by jerking the thumb of the right "A" hand back over the right shoulder. The sign for *refuse* may also be glossed as *won't.*

enjoy Executed with two hands rubbing the chest and stomach region, the sign means either the verb, *enjoy,* or the noun, *pleasure.* Executed with one hand, the sign means *like, please.*

FIG. **24.** *The thumbs-up marker adds emphasis to adjectives and adverbs so as to reflect the comparative and superlative, as in* **good, better,** *and* **best.**

best The *thumbs-up* intensifier, which is sometimes translated *chief,* converts an adjective or an adverb into a comparative or superlative in American Sign Language (see Fig. 24). The height of the final position of the sign indicates the degree to which the meaning is intensified. In this respect, American Sign Language is quite different from English, which has only two degrees of comparison, the comparative and the superlative, ordinarily indicated by means of suffixes, *-er* and *est.* American Sign Language operates within a continuum represented by the distance that the right hand can be raised comfortably at the right shoulder. There is only a superficial resemblance between the addition of *chief* to an adjective or adverb and the addition of an English suffix, *-er* or *est.* The sign, *chief,* can stand alone. One male student at a residential school was observed to assert, *My girl friend beautiful.* His friend replied, *Mine chief,* adding the intensifier, *chief,* to the first speaker's adjective. An alternative translation might be *Mine more so.* In any case, there is no American Sign Language counterpart for the English rule which requires a different construction for adjectives with three syllables: *more beautiful* rather than *beautifuler. Good, better* and *best* occur so frequently in normal conversation that they are well established in American Sign Language as conventional signs. The final position of *good,* which rests the back of the right hand in the left palm, is deleted as the intensifier sign, *chief,* is added so as to translate the comparative or superlative of English.

Spring time The sign for *Spring* is the same as the sign for *grow* (Fig. 25): the right "AND" hand is thrust up through the left "O" hand and opens into a "5." Signs for the other seasons are also derived from analogies. *Winter* is the same as *cold. Summer* wipes perspiration off the brow with the right "X" hand, a sign which may also mean *hot. Fall* is said to be derived from

FIG. **25.** *The sign for* **Spring** *also means* **grow.**

leaves falling from a tree: the right palm brushes alongside the base of the left forearm, which may represent a tree trunk (see Fig. 26). Since *Spring* already implies a time of the year, the sign for *time* may be omitted.

FIG. **26.** *The sign for* **Fall** *may be derived from the appearance of leaves falling off a tree.*

You know It has been mentioned previously that the subject matter of a discourse is generally established before there is any elaboration. By the same token, nouns often precede their adjectives. The time frame of a narrative is generally established at the outset, and the signer may use eye contact and questioning to insure that the receiver understands. *Cherry blossoms* are something special in Washington, D.C., but this might not be common knowledge. The signer may use a question like *You know* to make sure that he hasn't lost his receiver. He may expect a nod or some other sign of comprehension before proceeding. The importance of such sender-receiver signals during a conversation has been noted in the case of all languages. It may be that American Sign Language, for a variety of reasons, might require more frequent monitoring of receiver comprehension by senders. A visual language may be more easily disrupted by interruptions, since they may break eye contact. The signals that pass between signer and receiver to serve as indicators of understanding and rapport have not yet been thoroughly explored.

C-H-E-R-R-Y B-L-O-S-S-O-M-S There is a sign for *cherry,* the right thumb and index finger pinch the tip of the left index finger. But *Cherry Blossoms* is a technical term for Washingtonians in April, and the term may be spelled as a proper noun. Coupled with *You know,* the sentence is like a parenthetical expression. The next sentence may continue without fingerspelling.

Tree flower The sign for *tree* resembles a tree, with the arm representing the trunk and the "5" hand representing the branches. *Tree* may be pluralized by moving the vertical right arm toward the right across the front of the body as the sign is executed. *Flower* is derived from the act of smelling a flower. These two examples illustrate how unpredictable the motivation of a sign is likely to be. Some signs are derived from the physical appearance of the referent or a part of the referent. Others are derived from an activity that is associated with the use of the referent. It is almost impossible to predict from knowledge of a referent what the sign will be. This unpredictability of the source of a sign's motivation is one reason why the meaning of signs is not as transparent as one might think. Since the meaning of many signs appears to be plausible in retrospect, it might seem that someone with no knowledge of Sign Language might be able to guess correctly the meaning of a large number of signs. In actual fact it appears that about one-third of the signs in the American Sign Language lexicon are transparent enough that at least some people can guess what they mean some of the time. But another third of the signs are misleading in appearance, so that people are likely to be mistaken about their meaning, and another third are simply incomprehensible to people who do not know the language.

other flower The pronoun *other* moves the thumbs-up "A" hand off to the right. As an alternative, one could sign *small-tree flower,* suggesting flowering bushes. There is no sign for *small-tree* listed in any American Sign Language dictionary. But by using the right forearm to represent ground level, the sign for *tree* can be executed with a smaller trunk by placing the right arm against the horizontal left forearm with only the wrist and hand showing over the arm, thus representing a *bush* instead of a *tree*.

all-over The palm of the right hand is swept over an imaginery area in front of the body that encompasses a wide reach. The line of vision may follow the hand in a general way as if surveying the area that is broadly indicated. Eye contact with real or imaginary referents in a Sign Language discourse is an important adjunct to communicating manually. It attracts and holds receiver attention, it adds clarity to the referents indicated by means of manual signs, and it dramatizes the involvement of the signer with his message. The role of eye movements and eye contact, both with the receiver and with the region around the signer, merits more serious attention than it has thus far received from researchers.

true The sign *true, truly* is added for emphasis.

beautiful Just as the sign for *ugly* is derived from facial disfigurement, the sign for *beautiful* is linked to the notion of a pretty face: the fingertips of the "5" hand follow the perimeter of the face in a circular motion that ends with the "AND" configuration at the chin. A head jerk may accompany the sign for emphasis, *very beautiful*. Another way to add emphasis to the sign is to finish the sign with a flourish: the right hand is brought abruptly off to the right of the face, ending in a "5" configuration.

color There are a number of signs for *color* in use. One sign, probably derived from finger painting, rubs the tip of the right index finger in the left palm. Another wiggles the fingers of the right hand in front of the mouth. Still another is an initialized sign: the letter "C" is shaken back and forth in front of the right shoulder. Since the previous sign ended at the chin, there would be a slight preference for reasons of economy of effort to use the second sign

described above, assuming that it was known to all parties of the conversation.

Make sure This is an idiomatic expression in American Sign Language recommended by an informant as a good translation for English idiom, *no doubt about it*. *Make* is signed here the same as in *manufacture*. *Sure* is the same sign as *true, truly*, or *sure* may be signed with the right "B" hand, fingertips originating near the lips, shoved forward along the back of the left hand, palm down, in front of the body.

Washington beautiful place The sign for *place* is a more formal way to designate an area than the sweeping palm used earlier. In the initialized version of the sign, the "P" hands trace a circular area in a horizontal plane in front of the body. It is the initialized sign that is generally seen; however, it is likely that index fingers delineating an area were used in an earlier version. It seems safe to assume that most initialized signs are late additions to American Sign Language, coming in from the English language. Those that are not, had to have been used in French cognates by de l'Epee as a feature of his "Methodical Sign Language" and brought to this country intact by Thomas Hopkins Gallaudet and Laurent Clerc.

Some people The sign for *some* carves off a portion of the left palm with the edge of the right hand. Undoubtedly, it originally implied *some amount*, as in a part of a pie, rather than number. Perhaps because the English word can mean either *some amount* or *some number*, the sign can also apply to either circumstance. *People* is signed by moving the "P" hands alternately up and down or in a slight circular motion in front of the body.

complain This is a colorful sign: The bent "5" hands (or open "C" hands, whichever one prefers to call them) are struck alternately against the chest. A related sign places the tips of the fingers of both bent "5" hands against the chest as the body wriggles uncomfortably. The latter sign means *uncomfortable*. This sign, *uncomfortable*, is a clear example of the important role that the entire body plays in

Sign Languages. In spoken languages, such movements come under the category of kinesics. They would be treated as something else than language. But spoken languages are transmitted auditorially, and paralanguage or kinesics is transmitted visually. The channel separation makes the distinction somewhat easier to maintain. But in Sign Languages, paralanguage, kinesics, and signs are all transmitted visually, making distinctions between them extremely difficult if not entirely arbitrary.

government The right index finger is curled into the "X" configuration at the right temple and then touched to the side of the head. The same sign, with or without a person marker, can mean *governor*.

building The fingers of both "H" hands are stroked against one another's backs as they move upward in space in front of the body. The sign may be executed with "B" hands, and it may also be used as a verb, *build*. It has been suggested that the sign is derived from laying brick. Even if that is not correct, it still helps to conceptualize the movement if it is compared to brick laying.

all This sign helps to establish the previous noun as plural. It also emphasizes the scope of the charge.

seem The palm of the right hand is turned slightly toward the face at the right side of the head. The movement is made very deliberately, as if mental activity were accompanying the action. A related sign executed with two hands alternating means *compare*. An alternative Sign translation might use a sign which means *face, looks, appearance:* The right index finger traces a circle around the perimeter of the face. Combined with the sign for *same, like* (the "Y" hand moved back and forth), the meaning becomes *looks like, appears the same as.*

fake The sign intended by this gloss is the same as the sign for *false:* the bent "B" hand moves toward the left across the mouth. One is reminded of the proverbial American Indian expression for a liar as being a person who speaks with a forked tongue. Deaf persons characterize a liar as

someone who speaks sideways out of his mouth. A similar sign is made with the horizontal or vertical right index finger. Both signs may also translate the verb, *lie.*

Greek The American Sign Language sign for *Greek* is derived from the nose of the classic Greek profile: The right "G" hand is moved downward along the bridge of the nose, the thumb and index finger moving alongside the bony structure. There is a movement currently underway to develop an international Sign Language. One of the first emphases of this movement is to popularize the sign for each country that is used in that country. Thus, the sign that Greeks use for *Greece, Greek* would be recommended for American Sign Language users as well. This recommendation is likely to become effective in the near future. The National Association of the Deaf is participating in the project, and events like the World Congresses held by the World Deaf Federation and the International Games for the Deaf (sometimes called the Deaf Olympics) provide sufficient opportunities as well as incentives for deaf people from many nations to cooperate for the sake of better communication and better international relations. Since the subject of an international Sign Language has been broached, it is appropriate to point out that the Sign Languages currently in use around the world are sufficiently different from one another that deaf persons from different countries have considerable difficulty communicating with each other manually. If they succeed better than hearing people do under comparable circumstances, it is probably because deaf people are more accustomed to using pantomime and other nonverbal means of communicating.

temple The right "T" hand makes a small circle over the back of the left fist and then drops down to touch the back of the left fist. The sign is related to *church* (The right "C" hand is placed on the back of the left fist) and *institution:* (The right "I" hand makes a circle and then touches the back of the left fist or the left "I" hand). All three of these signs are initialized signs. The third one, *institution,* is a technical term in

American Sign Language for a state resi-.dential school for the deaf.

complain Instead of using a coordinate conjunction, *and,* the verb is repeated so as to generate a parallel construction.

go-out If the right hand is brought out forward from the body as it emerges from the left "C" hand, the sign becomes a verb, *go out.*

street, street The repetition implies pluralization. The signs for *street* provide a natural continuation of the movement begun in *out.*

night The right hand is tucked down over the horizontal left forearm. To make it a collective noun, applying to any and all nights rather than to one particular night, the arms may be moved toward the right in a horizontal plane as they are held in position (see Fig. 27).

FIG. **27.** *A lateral movement of the hands in the final position of the sign,* **night,** *makes it a collective noun,* **nights.**

not safe Either sign for *not* is permissible here, the thumb of the right "A" hand bumped under the chin, or the two open palms, facing outward, brought apart from an initial position of crossed wrists. Safe is signed by crossing the wrists as if bound and then pulling them apart. *S-A-F-E* may be fingerspelled for emphasis with the hand extended far out in front of the body so as to bring it closer to the receiver. The sign for *safe* also means *save.*

Maybe The two hands, palms up, are moved up and down alternately in front of the

body. The body posture and facial expression convey a feeling of indecision.

true Since this is a grudging admission, the shoulders might be hunched and the facial expression might simulate a yielding attitude.

but Here the attitude shifts to a more positive position. The sign *but* is related to one of the signs for *not, don't.* For *but,* the index fingers are crossed in front of the body and then brought apart to the sides. The sign also means *different, on the contrary.*

me still like The sign for *still* more commonly means *stay, remain, continue.* The right "Y" hand or both "Y" hands" move forward from the body at the waist. For *still,* the right "Y" hand may start at the shoulder facing the body and then twist outward as it is moved forward. *Like* may be signed by rubbing the right palm over the chest in the region of the stomach. It is related to the sign for *enjoy,* which is signed with both hands. The right palm circled over the heart means *please.* An alternative sign draws the right "F" hand, palm facing the body, forward from the body. The sign implies some sort of attraction associated with liking someone or something. Since *like* is generally signed with one hand, the sign for *still* would probably also be signed with one hand. It is as much a characteristic of American Sign Language as it is of any language that the elements that follow in a sentence may influence the form or structure of the elements that precede. In the case of spoken languages, it is the sounds of phonemes that are affected; in the case of Sign Languages it is the location of the signs, the orientation or configuration of the hands, and the movements of the hands that are affected. The locations, hand configurations, hand orientations, and movements of signs comprise some of the structural elements of signs, and they may serve as distinctive features. As Stokoe has proposed, such structure of Sign Languages may be analogous to the phonological structure of spoken languages.

All-right This is the same sign that also means *morally right.* The right hand, palm facing left and fingers pointing forward, is moved forward along the surface of the left palm. When signed as a concession, as in the present case, the wrist is often twisted so that the fingers trace an arc, pointing upward in their final position. As an alternative translation, the signer might fingerspell *O-K*.

have The fingertips of both hands are touched to the chest. This sign never translates the English auxiliary verb in the present perfect or past perfect tense. Anyone who uses it for that purpose is transmitting Signed English, not American Sign Language.

friend The "X" hands are interlocked by hooking the right index into the left. The hands then exchange places, as the left index finger hooks into the right.

many For emphasis, the sign *many* may follow the noun it modifies. Its effect is to pluralize *friend*.

in Washington The fingers of the right "B" hand are tucked into the left "O" hand for the preposition, *in*.

help The left "A" hand, thumb up, is raised upward by the fingers of the right palm. Initialized signs *assist* and *assistant* are derived from *help:* The thumb of the right "A" hand is touched to the underside of the left "A" hand, thumb up, one or more times. For *assistant* the person marker is generally added.

much The hands are drawn apart from one another in front of the body, palms facing. They may be cupped slightly as if containing *much*. The head may be cocked to the side slightly for emphasis as the signs *help much* are executed.

Judge This sign uses the same location and movement as *maybe*, but the hand configuration is "F" hands. This sign is one of the ways in which American Sign Language expresses some equivalent of the English *if* to introduce a conditional clause. Another is *idea*. *I-F* may be fingerspelled with an appropriate facial expression.

friend A plural is not necessary because of the next sign, *all*.

All move *All* is likely to be signed in a neutral position in front of the body, in the same location as *friend*. *Move*, however, must consider that the area in front of the body has been associated with Washington, D.C. That is where all of the beautiful flowering trees and shrubs were spread out. *Move* may begin in that area, but its final position must put the signer some distance away, perhaps off to the left from the front of the body.

Chicago The preposition *to* is not necessary; the verb *move* includes the directional indicator. The sign for *Chicago* is generally made by moving the right "C" hand downward in a waving motion in front of the right shoulder. In the present text it must be relocated to the terminal position of the sign for *move*. To accomplish this, it may be executed with the left hand instead of the right. Such relocation of signs is one way in which referents are localized relative to the signer for future reference or to distinguish them from other referents. In the present text, Washington, D.C., for which the signer has some obvious affinity, is located directly in front. Chicago, which is named somewhat at random as an alternative location, is placed off to the left. Now references to Chicago can be accompanied by body orientation or eye fixation toward that location, while references to Washington will continue to be made relative to the more natural position.

maybe me change This is the consequence of the condition expressed previously. *Change* is expressed by the relative movement and subsequent position of the two hands over against each other. It may be signed with "G" or "X" hands. The right hand begins below the left, palms facing, and the hands are interchanged, the right for the left, so that the right hand is above the left in the final position. Of course, since left-handed signing is not forbidden, the left hand may begin below the right as a variation in execution.

like Chicago These signs are the same as described previously, except that the sign for Chicago might still be dislocated off to the left.

But seem not happen The first three signs are the same as were ·used previously.

Happen begins with the two "G" hands, palms up, in front of the body, and turns them over abruptly. If the same sign is moved forward from the body as the hands are turned over, it means *during, while.*

Me still think This construction is identical to an earlier phrase, *Me still like. Think* is signed by tracing a small circle on the forehead. A number of signs depicting mental activity are signed on the forehead: *know, forget, stupid, smart,* etc. Although large numbers of signs derive no meaning at all from the location in which they are signed, some locations sometimes add semantic content to the signs that are executed there.

Washington, D.C. nice place *Nice* is the same sign as *clean:* The right palm scrapes across the upturned left palm in front of the body. *Place* can be executed in front of the body, which is where Washington, D.C., is located for the purpose of the discussion.

Me always feel *Always* is signed by a clockwise circle (from the signer's vantage point) executed below the level of the right shoulder on the right side of the body. The extent to which the movement of signs depends on human anatomy can be seen from the direction of the circles that are executed in Sign Languages. The circle is ordinarily made in the direction that is easiest, and this depends on which hand is used, left, right, or both, and how the palm is turned relative to the body. The sign *feel* strokes the chest with the tip of the middle finger of the right hand. The same finger is used with a number of signs implying sensation or emotion: *touch, sick, hate, excited, naked,* etc. Just as the location of a sign may sometimes contribute to its semantic content, as in mental signs, so also the hand configuration of a sign can serve as evidence for its relation to other signs with related meanings.

same home The sign for *same* is the same one that was used previously for *like,* the right "Y" hand is moved back and forth with two clear stops, one at either side of the body. The sign may have originally imitated the measuring of two items with the span of the thumb and little finger and finding them to be the *same.*

VOCABULARY

1. again (HH-352, TO-191)
2. all (HH-494, TO-193)
3. all night (HH-308, TO-187)
4. all over (see text)
5. all right (HH-302, TO-60)
6. always (HH-370, TO-83)
7. America (HH-485, TO-166)
8. anyway (HH-169, TO-196)
9. appearance (HH-152, TO-85)
10. assist (HH-495, TO-526)
11. assistant (HH-495, TO-528)
12. Autumn (HH-299, TO-283)
13. beautiful (HH-152, TO-233)
14. best (TO-506)
15. better (HH-342, TO-505)
16. blossoms (fingerspell)
17. build (HH-159, TO-352)
18. building (HH-159, TO-352)
19. bush (see text)
20. but (HH-164, TO-26)
21. California (see text)
22. can (HH-72, TO-155)
23. change (HH-484, TO-663)
24. cherry (fingerspell)
25. Chicago (see text)
26. chief (HH-270, TO-128)
27. church (HH-213, TO-481)
28. city (HH-154, TO-351)
29. cold (HH-272, TO-158)
30. color (TO-149)
31. compare (HH-363, TO-198)
32. complain (HH-300, TO-150)
33. Detroit (see text)
34. different (HH-164, TO-27)
35. don't (HH-50, TO-43)
36. during (HH-174, TO-102)
37. enjoy (HH-42, TO-255)
38. excited (HH-493, TO-397)
39. face (HH-152, TO-85)
40. fake (HH-440, TO-224)
41. Fall (HH-299, TO-283)
42. false (HH-440, TO-224)
43. feel (HH-442, TO-388)
44. finish (HH-214, TO-174)
45. flower (HH-125, TO-234)
46. forget (HH-120, TO-517)

47. friend (HH-314, TO-638)
48. go (HH-312, TO-114)
49. go-out (HH-30, TO-15)
50. gold (HH-387)
51. good (HH-342, TO-259)
52. government (HH-256)
53. governor (HH-256)
54. Greece (TO-652)
55. Greek (TO-652)
56. grow (HH-364, TO-487)
57. happen (HH-174, TO-228)
58. hate (HH-466, TO-398)
59. have (HH-292, TO-268)
60. help (HH-495, TO-526)
61. home (HH-489, TO-241)
62. hot (HH-441, TO-634)
63. house (HH-154, TO-350)
64. I have been to (see text)
65. I have visited (see text)
66. in (HH-242, TO-14)
67. indifference (HH-169, TO-196)
68. institution (HH-136, TO-417)
69. It makes no difference (HH-169, TO-196)
70. judge (HH-306, TO-559)
71. know (HH-14, TO-206)
72. lie (HH-440)
73. like, enjoy (HH-42, TO-255)
74. like, same (see text)
75. looks (HH-152, TO-85)
76. make (HH-210, TO-298)
77. manufacture (HH-210, TO-298)
78. many (HH-34, TO-657)
79. maybe (HH-19, TO-51)
80. me (HH-192, TO-2)
81. morally right (HH-302, TO-60)
82. more so (HH-270, TO-128)
83. move (HH-286, TO-252)
84. much (HH-473, TO-167)
85. naked (HH-294, TO-607)
86. never (HH-390, TO-45)
87. nevertheless (HH-169, TO-196)
88. New Orleans (see text)
89. nice (HH-112, TO-48)
90. night (HH-308, TO-186)
91. no (HH-50, TO-43)

92. not (HH-249, TO-44)
93. often (HH-352, TO-192)
94. on the contrary (HH-164, TO-26)
95. other (HH-348, TO-91)
96. people (HH-320, TO-427)
97. Philadelphia (see text)
98. Pittsburgh (see text)
99. place (HH-44, TO-433)
100. please (HH-42, TO-255)
101. pleasure (HH-42, TO-255)
102. refuse (HH-58, TO-38)
103. remain (HH-278, TO-647)
104. right morally (HH-302, TO-60)
105. safe (HH-467, TO-294)
106. same (see text)
107. save (HH-467, TO-294)
108. say no (HH-380, TO-42)
109. seem (HH-363, TO-203)
110. sick (HH-20, TO-387)
111. smart (HH-239, TO-392)
112. some (HH-60, TO-61)
113. Spring (HH-364, TO-487)

114. stay (HH-278, TO-647)
115. still, yet (HH-278, TO-645)
116. street (HH-412, TO-344)
117. stupid (HH-389, TO-588)
118. Summer (HH-441, TO-634)
119. sure (HH-291, TO-219)
120. temple (HH-213, TO-481)
121. think (HH-226, TO-79)
122. time (HH-187, TO-595)
123. touch (HH-458, TO-590)
124. touring the countryside (see text)
125. tree (HH-150, TO-284)
126. true (HH-291, TO-219)
127. ugly (HH-171, TO-633)
128. uncomfortable (HH-300)
129. visit (HH-227, TO-300)
130. Washington, D.C. (TO-443)
131. while (HH-174, TO-102)
132. Winter (HH-272, TO-158)
133. won't (HH-58, TO-38)
134. you (HH-403, TO-3)

EXERCISES

Sign the following sentences and provide an English translation.

1. Some people enjoy best Spring; me different; me think Fall better.

2. During Summer flowers grow all over; Winter change; all bare.

3. Tree grow in New Orleans, tree grow in New York: different.

4. Me refuse stay home; go out, visit friend.

5. Washington in Spring beautiful, in Summer often uncomfortable.

6. You always complain, complain, complain; finish; not nice.

7. Me think California beautiful, best place in America.

8. Some people refuse live city; me think different; like city.

9. Me go, go, go New York many times; again, again, again visit. Enjoy.

10. Governor live in house beautiful.

Lesson Six

ENGLISH ORIGINAL

A Seaside Vacation

A lot of people think that you need a lot of money to take a vacation on the seashore, but that's not true. If you are willing to give up some of the comforts of home, you can spend a week or two on the shore very inexpensively. I used to vacation regularly on the shore with my wife and three children. We lived in a tent. We cooked our meals on a small stove and kept our food in an ice box. For a shower we wrapped some old shower curtains around four posts that we had tied down. All during the day we left water standing in buckets in the sun, and at night we would have warm water to wash up. Most of the time we would drive into town and buy food at a grocery store. But sometimes we would take some left over chicken wings and use them for bait to catch some crabs. They were delicious. It was a simple life, a big change from life in the city. That is why we liked it so much.

SIGN LANGUAGE GLOSS

Vacation Near Ocean

Many people think (pause) vacation near ocean (pause) need money much. Not. You have nice house, big, comfortable? Nice house move ocean, true expensive. Nice house give-up, leave-behind. You can go near ocean, stay one-week, stay two-weeks, cheap. Me ago vacation near ocean regularly. Wife children three group-go. Live where? Tent. Cook with small box C-A-M-P S-T-O-V-E. Food keep in other box little-bit big. Go downtown buy ICE put-in. Food put-in. Keep fine. Want bath? Get post four. Stick-in-ground. Have old shower curtain. Wrap-around. Tie-down stake. There. Want hot shower? Morning get bucket one, two, three, many you want. Water pour-in, fill. All-day let. Night, look; water warm. Pour-over-head. Nice bath. Need food, most time drive town near, buy from food store. Sometimes have chicken left, use for BAIT, catch crab. Truly delicious. That life ago very plain. City life opposite. Why much enjoy? From city, big change.

Many The "A" hands, palms up, are flicked upward and opened into "5" hands one or more times. One hand only may be used. The same sign executed with one hand and held in the final position with a questioning expression may mean *How many?* or *How much?* in the sense of *How much money?*

people The singular, *person,* is signed by drawing both "P" hands downward in front of the body as if outlining another person's body. The initialization is not necessary; just the hands, palms facing may be used. The plural, *people,* is indicated by moving the two "P" hands up and down alternately in front of the body or forming small circles toward the body as the "P" hands are moved up and down alternately in front of the body.

think The index finger is touched to the forehead. Here, the finger may be jabbed at the forehead somewhat emphatically to indicate that the thought is the main idea of the first sentence, and it is going to be contradicted. The pause following *think* also has the purpose of eliciting additional rapport with the receiver, who is going to be told what it is that people think.

vacation The thumbs of the "5" hands are touched to the shoulders several times or the "5" hands are held with the thumbs touching the shoulders as the fingers are wiggled. It is reported that the sign imitates someone sticking his thumbs under his suspenders and enjoying sedentary leisure.

near ocean The preposition, *near,* uses the palm of the left hand, facing the body, as a point of reference. The right hand, palm also facing the body, is moved toward the left, and the back of the right hand is stopped *near* the palm of the left. With the addition of a *person marker* the sign is used to indicate *neighbor. Ocean* is motivated by waves, the two hands form waves moving forward or off to the left in front of the body. The location of the sign for *ocean* may influence the location of the sign for

near. For example, if *ocean* is to be signed somewhat distant from the body so as to indicate that it is somewhat far away, then *near* may also be executed farther from the body than is typical.

need The curved index finger of the right hand, palm down, is brought downward in front of the body. If it is brought downward once, forcefully, it is likely to be translated "must" or "ought." If it is brought downward in a brief movement that is repeated several times, it is likely to be translated "need" or "should."

money The back of the right "AND" hand is tapped into the left palm several times. If the right "AND" hand is pressed into the palm of the left hand once and then moved forward as if extending it toward an imaginary person, the sign means *buy.*

much The two cupped hands are brought apart from each other in front of the body. Since the left palm was just used to indicate money, it is likely that the sign will be executed vertially instead of horizontally, as if the money is piled up in front of the signer.

You The index finger is pointed directly forward at the receiver.

have The fingertips of both hands are touched to the chest. This is *have* in the sense of *possess.* This sign does not translate the English helping verb, *have.*

nice house The left hand is held, palm up, in front of the body, and the palm of the right hand is scraped across it as the right hand is moved forward from the body. The sign also means *clean.* If it is repeated several times as the hands are moved around in front of the body, the sign means *clean up.* The sign for *house* is motivated by the shape of the roof and walls. This sentence, *You have nice house big comfortable,* is a question, and a questioning expression should be maintained throughout the execution of the sentence. Since the receiver's response is presumed to be "Yes," the signer may nod frequently as the sentence is signed as if to say, "You do have a nice, big, comfortable house, don't you?"

big The "L" hands with curved index fingers are brought apart, left and right, in front of the body.

comfortable The palms of both hands are rubbed alternately over the backs of each hand. It has been suggested that the sign is motivated from the action of rubbing hands to keep them warm, as before a fire. This is the end of the question, and one more nod may follow with raised eyebrows to elicit the expected affirmative response.

nice house It is important that the distance between the house and the ocean be reflected in the positioning of these signs. If the *ocean,* previously, was signed off to the left sort of far from the body, then *house* can be signed right in front of the body. If *ocean* was signed near the body perhaps slightly off to the left, then *house* should probably be signed off to the right a bit. This sets the stage for repeating the signs *nice house* exactly where they were signed previously. The reason for this is the next verb, *move.*

move This sign is executed in such a way that its initial position is directly over the

nice, comfortable house and so that its final position is at the previously established location for the ocean (see Fig. 28). The suggestion is that the house is being picked up by the sign for *move* and transported to the ocean. The localization of *house* and *ocean* is an important feature of this translation and helps to reduce any ambiguity that would result if they were not localized. As long as the location of the sign is exactly the same both times, the mere suggestion of a wave or two is sufficient. This statement, too, can be construed as a question, "Would you want to move your nice house to the ocean?" In that case, a questioning facial expression would be held as the four signs were executed. Such facial expressions link signs together syntactically and provide an important source of structure in Sign Language sentences. The questioning expression would change to one of conviction as the next two signs are executed.

true expensive *True* is added for emphasis. *Expensive* is a compound derived from *money* and a sign that also intensifies other signs and may be glossed as *wow* or *phew! Money + phew = expensive.*

Nice house give-up Again, the signs *nice house* should be signed exactly over the

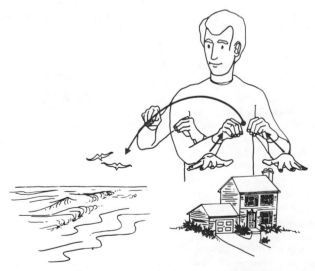

FIG. 28. Move *is an example of a class of verbs whose execution takes into account the localization of referenced elements in the sentence.*

same location as previously. Then, the sign *give-up* is signed directly over the house, and the object of the verb will be indicated by the location where the verb is signed. The sign for *give-up* begins with "A" hands, palms down, and as both hands are raised upward the hands are opened as if relinquishing their contents. The head may be turned away in addition, as if to indicate a loss of interest in whatever is being given up.

leave-behind Both hands, palms facing, are brought forcefully downward as if discarding whatever is between them. Again, this sign is executed directly over the location of the "Nice house" so as to indicate that it is the object.

You can go near ocean The sequence of these signs is somewhat arbitrary. Depending on the desired emphasis, one might sign, *go near ocean you can* or *near ocean go you can*. The verb, *go*, should be signed off to the left where the ocean has been located. The head may be nodded emphatically as the sign for *can* is executed.

Stay one week The sign for *stay*, the right "Y" hand moved forward from the body, palm down, may also be executed toward the ocean to indicate that staying at the ocean is being discussed. The numeral, *one*, for *one-week* need not be displayed prominently, since the sign for *week* is generally modulated with an indication of how many weeks are meant.

two-weeks In this case the numeral *two* is formed on the right hand as the sign for *week* is executed, thus indicating the number of weeks implied. The idea here is that you can stay for one or two weeks. Both sentences, *Stay one week* and *Stay two-week* would probably be signed in the general direction of the ocean with very similar style and emphasis.

cheap The left hand is held with the palm facing the right. The right hand, palm up, is turned over, palm down, and brushed past the face of the left palm, as if scraping off anything that was left there. This sign often means *cheap* in a derogatory sense, but, as in English, it can also be used for *inexpensive*.

Me ago If the intention is to indicate that it was a long time ago that this happened, both hands may be moved alternately back over the right shoulder several times, with each movement successively farther back. On the other hand, if the past event is recent, one backward toss of the right hand, palm toward the rear or palm facing left and slightly to the rear, should be sufficient.

near ocean regularly *Regularly* is signed by repeatedly striking the right fist, index finger extended and pointing forward, on top of the left fist, index finger also extended and pointing forward. Typically both hands move forward slightly or in an upward direction as the striking is repeated.

Wife This is a compound: *female + marry = wife.* By the same token, *male + marry = husband. Female* strokes the thumb of the right "A" hand along the right cheek or jaw. *Male* closes the right "5" hand to the "AND" configuration in front of the forehead. *Marry* clasps the two hands together.

children This sign is said to be motivated by patting children of differing stature on the head. The fingertips of both hands pat imaginary children on the head as they move to each side on front of the body.

three The numeral, *three*, would be signed very quickly after the sign for *children* so as to make it plain that the *three* applied to the children.

FIG. 29. *The addition of a movement to the sign,* **group,** *has the effect of supplying a verb,* **group go.**

66

group-go The rhythm here would make it plain that the group included the signer, the wife, and the three children. *Wife* (pause) *children three* (pause) *group-go*. The latter sign, *group-go* (Fig. 29), illustrates how easily a sign can have a verb attached in American Sign Language by executing it with a movement. Even prepositions, such as *with* and *near* may become verbs, such as *accompany* and *approach*. In the present case, the sign *group* references the family, and moving the sign to the location of the ocean has the effect of indicating that the group comprising the family is going to the ocean. The object need not be repeated, since the direction of the movement references the ocean as the destination.

Live The "A" or "L" hands are drawn up the chest.

where There are two equally appropriate signs for *where* in American Sign Language. One is similar to the sign for *here*, only it is executed with a questioning expression. The two hands, palms up, are moved from side to side in front of the body in a manner that is similar to a natural quizzical gesture. The second sign uses the upright right index finger in front of the right shoulder and waggles it back and forth, also a natural gesture for *Huh? Where? Who?* The informality of the present text would probably argue for the second alternative.

Tent The sign for *tent* is similar to the sign for *house*: the outline of the peaked roof is traced with the hands. The only difference is the hand configuration: *House* is signed with the open palms; *tent* is signed with "V" hands.

Cook This sign is derived from turning flap jacks on a stove; the left hand is held, palm up, in front of the body to represent a grill, and the right hand is placed palm down, palm up, palm down, palm up in the left hand as if it were something being turned in a pan. A related sign holds the left hand similarly and the right "AND" hand, palm up, is opened up to a "5" hand under the left hand in a representation of a flame that is heating the grill.

with Both fists are placed side by side touching at the knuckles.

small box The approximate size of a camp stove is indicated "fisherman style" with the palms of the hands. It is not necessary that the size be exactly represented, since the intent is to imply that it was a small appliance that was used. *Box* is simply indicated by the hands marking the length first, palms facing, and then the width, right palm facing back of left hand. Again, the proportions of a camp stove may be roughly approximated, but precision is not important.

C-A-M-P S-T-O-V-E It is recommended that C-A-M-P S-T-O-V-E be fingerspelled.

Food The sign for *food* is the same as the sign for *eat*. The context will indicate when the sign is a noun and when it is a verb.

keep The right "K" hand, palm left, is tapped on top of the left "K" hand, palm right. This same hand configuration and orientation, when circled in a horizontal plane in front of the body, is the common sign for a *dormitory supervisor* at a residential school for the deaf. The same sign for *keep* executed with the hands closer to the face and with the fingers pointing more in an upward direction may mean *careful* provided the context and facial expression are appropriate.

in other box The preposition *in* is signed by tucking the fingertips of the right "AND" hand into the left "O" hand, palm right. *Other* is signed with the right "A" hand, thumb up, swung in an arc off to the right. Box is signed as previously except for some slight accommodation to differences in size in the real objects.

little-bit big The sign for *little-bit* is, perhaps, a natural gesture in which the thumb nail of the right hand shaves off imaginary particles off the right index finger. The sign is often used to indicate a comparison. Given a series of objects, ranging from small to large, the smallest one would be small. The objects next to the smallest would be a *little-bit small*. The objects next to the largest would be a *little-bit big*. The largest would be big. In the present context, a box that is a *little-bit big* is one that is slightly larger than the stove.

Go downtown The sign for *go* may be made very casually with the index finger or

67

hand moved in the general direction where one is going or just forward from the body. *Downtown* is signed like *city:* the fingertips of both hands are touched together several times as if to indicate the roof lines of many buildings. For *city* the hands may move from left to right in front of the body as if designating a skyline. For *downtown* that is less likely; the hands are touched together at the fingertips as they are held in front of the body.

buy I-C-E *Buy* is derived from *money.* The back of the right "AND" hand is placed in the upturned palm of the left and then brought forward from the body as if presenting the money to someone. *I-C-E* is likely to be fingerspelled, although *frozen water* may also serve.

put-in This may be executed as a natural gesture which will take into consideration the size and weight of the block of ice.

box The walls of the box will be indicated as previously, but they will be placed so as to enclose the block of ice that has just been put inside.

food put-in Food is signed as before. The movement associated with *put-in* will be the same as before, executed where the "Box" has been placed relative to the signer. But the hands may be shaped differently, reflecting the fact that it is groceries that are now being put into the box instead of a block of ice. This is one reason why the object is likely to precede the verb in the present translation. As an alternative, the left "C" hand, palm down, may represent the container, and the sign *put-in* may be executed by moving the fingertips of the right "AND" hand toward the left hand. This choice allows some symmetry in the execution of the two phrases, *I-C-E put-in food put-in.*

keep fine *Keep* is signed as before. *Fine* is signed by touching the thumb of the right "5" hand to the chest several times. A smug facial expression may support the notion that there was no problem with keeping food in this way. *Fine* is the common answer to the polite question, "How are you?"

Want bath *Want* draws the two "CLAW" hands, palms up, toward the body. *Bath* is signed by rubbing the two fists up and down on the chest as if rubbing soap on the body. *Shower* is signed by using the right "AND" hand, fingers pointing downward above the head, opening into "5" hands so as to imitiate the spray of water coming out of the shower head.

Get The two "5" hands are brought toward the body, the right hand slightly above the left, ending as clenched fists, the right on top of the left, in front of the body.

pole four There is no standard sign for *pole,* but if circles are formed with the thumb and index fingers of both hands and these are drawn apart from each other as if tracing the outline of a *pole,* this is a satisfactory imitiation. The four fingers are held up to indicate the number of posts needed. As a variation, the sign for *pole* may be signed four times, and the numeral *four* may still be added as a redundant message. If *pole* is signed four times, it is likely that the four poles will be localized in a square as a suggestion as to their eventual arrangement.

Stick-in-ground This may be signed by using the right index finger pointed downward and jabbed into the imaginary ground. It would be likely to be repeated four times so as to indicate the square arrangement required for a shower enclosure made with four poles. As an alternative, the hands may hold imaginary poles which are driven into the ground by hand in a square arrangement.

Have old shower curtain For *have* the tips of the fingers of both hands are touched to the chest. *Old* is signed by tracing the outline of a flowing beard in a waving movement down from the chin with the right "C" hand. *Shower* is signed as previously, imitiating the spray of water from the shower head. *Curtain* may be indicated by drawing the fingers of both "5" hands, palms down, downward in front of the body one or more times so as to portray a curtain or drape. The entire expression is signed as a single phrase without pausing between the signs.

Wrap-around There is no standard sign for *wrap* or *wrap-around.* The way in which the sign is executed will depend on what is wrapped around what. In this case, four poles have already been stuck in the ground relative to the signer's body, and the shower curtain that is to be wrapped around them has already been indicated. All that needs to be done is for the right "5" hand to make a circle around the four poles so as to indicate that they are now providing an enclosure. To indicate that the curtain completely surrounds the poles, the right "5" hand may begin its circular movement from the fingertips of the left "5" hand. In effect, the signer is building the enclosure right before the eyes of the receiver, using materials that have first been carefully designated.

Tie-down, stake This action sequence would be pantomimed. The signer would imitate the actions associated with tying a rope to the top of a pole, extend the rope down to the ground, and then drive an imaginary stake in the ground with an imaginary hammer. The entire sequence might be repeated four times in four different directions, with each rope attached to one of the poles. Notice that the sequence of setting the poles, wrapping the shower curtain, and staking the entire enclosure follows the sequence that is appropriate for setting up and securing such a device. Sign Languages often follow what has been termed a "narrative sequence" in describing events as they have transpired.

There This is also a natural gesture; the right hand, palm up, is moved downward in front of the body and brought to a full stop exactly where the shower enclosure has been set up.

Want hot shower Since the signs for *hot* and *shower* require only the right hand, the left hand may retain its final position of *want* while the next two signs are executed. For *hot* the "CLAW" hand is placed with the palm toward the mouth and turned outward with a quick twist of the wrist. The mouth may be opened while the sign is executed. An alternate sign uses the middle finger of the right hand as the main feature of the right hand configuration; the location and movement are the same. The phrase is marked with a questioning expression that spans all three signs. At the

end, the sign for *want* may be repeated, as if to say, "Do you want a hot shower? Do you?"

Morning The left arm is held horizontally in front of the body, representing the horizon and the right arm is brought up from under it, bending at the elbow, as if the sun were appearing in the morning.

get bucket Get is signed as previously. Bucket is indicated by holding an imaginary bucket by the handle waist high.

one, two, three, many you want The numerals are raised tentatively as if any one of them would be as acceptable as any other. *Many you want* may be signed either as a question, with arched eyebrows, or as a statement, with a neutral facial expression.

Water pour-in *Water* is signed by touching a "W" to the lips. *Pour-in* is a natural gesture, although it may be signed with the right "A" hand, thumb extended, with the thumb representing a spout out of which the water is poured.

Fill The left "O" or "C" hand is held with the opening at the top, and the right hand, palm down, is scraped over the top, moving toward the left. The sign may be repeated two or three times, and the sign may be executed in such a way that each execution fills another bucket, with the buckets lined up in a row.

All-day The sign for *all-day* is the same as the sign for day, except it is executed more slowly and deliberately, making sure that the sun really goes all the way across the sky and reaches the opposite horizon. As in *morning,* the left arm provides a marker for the horizon, and the right hand, elbow resting in the left hand, is moved in an arc across the imaginary sky. The index finger may be extended as the sign is executed. In an alternate version, the sign for *day* goes from a position parallel to the left arm and is raised upward, moving toward the right.

Let This sign also is the same sign that was used previously for *leave-behind.* Here, the sign may be executed down toward the imaginary buckets on the ground.

Night The horizon is indicated as before, with the horizontal left arm. Here the right hand is tucked over the right wrist so that the fingertips point downard.

look The right "V" hand is placed near the eyes with the fingers pointing toward the eyes. The hand is then turned outward so that the fingers point directly toward the ground where the filled buckets are located.

water warm The sign for *warm* is similar to the sign for *hot*. The cupped right hand is held near the mouth, palm toward the fingers are gradually unfurled and the hand slowly opened as it moves upward and outward from the mouth. The sign may be derived from the warmth of human breath. The left index finger may point downward to the imaginary buckets as the right hand signs *water warm*.

Pour-over-head This is a natural gesture; an imaginary bucket is held above the head, and its contents are poured over the signer's head.

Nice bath *Nice* is signed by holding the left hand, palm up, and by stroking the right palm over it as the right hand moves off to the right. *Bath* is signed as indicated previously.

Need food *Need* is signed as before. *Food* is signed by moving the fingertips of the right "AND" hand toward the mouth. The same sign is used for the verb, *eat*.

most time *Most* is signed by holding the left fist, thumb up, in front of the body, and grazing the knuckles of the left fist with the right fist, thumb up, as the right fist is raised upward in front of the body. *Time* is signed by touching the right index finger to the back of the left wrist, where a watch is generally worn.

drive *Drive* and *car* are both signed by imitating the turning of a steering wheel.

town The fingertips of the two hands are touched together several times in front of the body. The same sign in other contexts may mean *downtown*. It is derived from the sign for *house*, but it is not merely a repetition of the sign for *house*. There is also an abbreviation of its movement.

buy The verb, *buy*, is derived from the sign for *money*. The back of the right "AND" hand is placed in the upturned left palm and moved forward as if presenting it to a salesperson.

from food store *From* is signed by holding the left index finger up as a point of reference and then drawing the curved right index finger away from it toward the signer's body. *Food* is signed as previously. *Store* is signed by shaking the fingers of both "AND" hands briefly in front of the body. The sign is said to be derived from a salesperson holding a garment up and shaking it so as to display it to a customer. The sign also means *sell*. It may have a negative connotation, as in *peddle*.

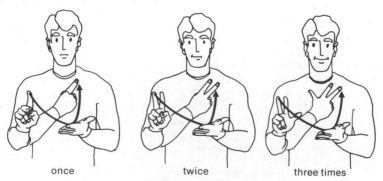

once   twice   three times

FIG. **30.** *The ordinal adjectives or adverbs are signed similarly to one set of ordinal numerals, that is, with a hooking movement in the shape of a "J" in front of the right shoulder; in the adverbs and adjectives, however, the fingertip of the right hand strikes across the left palm.*

Sometimes If the right index finger is stroked downward and touched to the upturned left palm and then raised upward again, the sign means *once*. The same sign executed with a numeral *two* on the right hand means *twice*. If the same sign is executed more slowly and deliberately, and the movement repeated several times, as if to say *once, once, once,* etc., the meaning becomes *sometimes, occasionally.*

have The fingertips of the both hands are touched to the chest. One hand only may also be used.

chicken The right index finger and thumb are touched together several times at the mouth, representing a chicken's beak. The citation form of the sign may also include pecking into the upturned left palm.

left The two hands, palms facing, are lowered with a jerk in front of the body, fingers pointing slightly downward. The sign is a variation on the sign for *leave, abandon.* The latter is signed more forcefully and off to the side of the body.

use The right "U" hand is circled over the back of the left fist.

for B-A-I-T *For* is signed with the right index finger touched to the forehead and then turned forward from the forehead so that the fingertip points slightly outward. *B-A-I-T* is fingerspelled.

catch The right hand makes a snatching motion around in front of the body. The left arm may be used as a support for the right hand so as to present a handle such as is found on a crab net.

crab Both "V" hands, palms down, make pinching movements as the hands move forward from the body. The arms may be curved slightly so as to represent the claws.

Truly This is the same sign as *true*, used previously.

delicious The middle fingertip of the right hand is touched to the lips, and then the right hand is brought forward from the mouth with a flourish. This sign is related to the sign for *taste*, which simply touches the middle finger of the right hand to the lips. Another sign for *delicious* that may be seen occasionally touches the right index finger to the right side of the neck below the jaw and twists it slightly with an appropriate facial expression. The facial expression supports the notion that this is a pleasurable sensation.

life This is the same sign as the verb, *live.* Either "A" hands or "L" hands may be used to execute it.

ago The right and left hands, palms facing, are moved backward over the right shoulder in alternative motions. The more often the movements are executed and the farther back the hands are moved, the more distant in the past the event is presumed to be.

very plain *Very* is signed by drawing both "V" hands, palms facing, apart from each other in front of the body. *Plain* may be signed by gently pressing the palms of both "5" hands downward, as if to emphasize the calm nature of the life that was being described. As an alternative, the sign for *clean, nice,* may be used or the sign for *naked, bare, empty.* Of the choices, *calm* would appear to capture the flavor the best.

City This is the same sign as was used previously for *town*, except that it might be executed more frequently or the hands may move across the front of the body so as to indicate the larger size of the city.

life opposite *Life* is signed as before. *Opposite* is signed similarly to *different,* but for greater emphasis the fingertips of both hands point directly toward each other and then the hands are jerked abruptly apart. Both hands may twist at the wrist for additional emphasis as the sign is executed.

Why The right hand is held in front of the forehead with the palm facing the forehead. The hand is then dipped down so that the fingertips graze the forehead and outward from the forehead as the hand changes to a "Y" configuration.

much The hands are held in front of the body, palms facing, and they are brought apart from each other. The sign for *very* is an initialized version of this sign. *Large* is signed the same way, but with "L" hands.

enjoy The palms of both hands are rubbed simultaneously on the chest and stomach. A questioning facial expression is likely to be held across the three signs, *Why much enjoy?* not only to mark this as a question but also to set boundaries on the clause.

From city *From* and *city* are both signed as described previously. The facial expression is likely to change with *from* to signal a new clause.

big This sign is derived from *much:* The "L" hands with curved thumbs and index fingers are held in front of the body, palms facing, and they are brought apart from each other.

change The "X" hands are held, palms facing, with the right hand above the left. The positions of the hands are reversed with twists of both wrists, so that the left "X" hand is on top of the right in the final position.

1. abandon (HH-276, TO-175)
2. accompany (HH-476, TO-19)
3. ago (HH-118, TO-205)
4. all day (HH-250, TO-182)
5. approach (HH-163, TO-365)
6. bait (fingerspell)
7. bare (HH-294, TO-607)
8. bath (HH-99, TO-117)
9. big (HH-473, TO-429)
10. box (TO-358)
11. bucket (see text)
12. buy (HH-447, TO-66)
13. camp stove (fingerspell)
14. can (HH-72, TO-155)
15. car (HH-375, TO-160)
16. careful (HH-304, TO-308)
17. catch (TO-605)
18. change (HH-484, TO-663)
19. cheap (TO-68)
20. chicken (HH-111)
21. children (HH-40, TO-147)
22. city (HH-154, TO-351)
23. clean (HH-112, TO-48)
24. clean up (HH-112, TO-48)
25. comfortable (HH-49, TO-57)
26. cook (HH-339, TO-55)
27. crab (see text)
28. curtain (see text)
29. delicious (TO-391)
30. dormitory supervisor (see text)
31. downtown (HH-154, TO-351)
32. drive (HH-375, TO-160)
33. eat (HH-491, TO-235)
34. empty (HH-294, TO-607)
35. enjoy (HH-42, TO-255)
36. expensive (HH-447 + 81, TO-69)
37. female (HH-500, TO-106)
38. fill (HH-225, TO-535)
39. fine (HH-444, TO-135)
40. food (HH-491, TO-235)
41. for (HH-404, TO-18)
42. four (TO-p. 4)
43. from (HH-16, TO-33)
44. frozen (HH-365, TO-414)
45. get (HH-455, TO-604)
46. give up (HH-274, TO-589)
47. go (HH-312, TO-114)
48. group (HH-421, TO-412)
49. group go (see text)
50. have (HH-292, TO-268)
51. hot (HH-498, TO-136)
52. house (HH-154, TO-350)
53. how many? (HH-34, TO-658)
54. how much (HH-34, TO-658)
55. huh? (HH-183, TO-28)
56. husband (HH-238 + 248, TO-409)
57. ice (fingerspell)
58. in (HH-242, TO-14)
59. inexpensive (TO-68)
60. keep (HH-304, TO-309)
61. large (HH-473, TO-429)
62. leave behind (HH-276, TO-175)
63. left (HH-276, TO-175)
64. let (HH-276, TO-175)
65. life (HH-446, TO-120)
66. little bit (TO-655)
67. live (HH-446, TO-119)
68. look (HH-413, TO-209)
69. male (HH-238, TO-105)
70. many (HH-34, TO-657)
71. marry (HH-248, TO-405)
72. me (HH-192, TO-2)
73. money (HH-447, TO-63)
74. morning (HH-228, TO-183)
75. most (HH-301, TO-128)
76. move (HH-286, TO-252)
77. much (HH-473, TO-167)
78. naked (HH-294, TO-607)
79. near (HH-163, TO-367)
80. need (HH-62, TO-628)
81. neighbor (HH-163 + 18, TO-367)
82. nice (HH-112, TO-48)
83. night (HH-308, TO-186)
84. not (HH-249, TO-44)
85. occasionally (HH-471, TO-468)
86. ocean (HH-405, TO-343)
87. old (HH-110, TO-485)
88. once (HH-471, TO-468)
89. one (TO-p. 4)
90. one week (HH-326, TO-462)
91. opposite (HH-45, TO-323)

92. other (HH-348, TO-92)
93. peddle (HH-78, TO-242)
94. people (HH-320, TO-427)
95. person (HH-18, TO-426)
96. person marker (HH-18)`
97. phew (HH-81)
98. plain (see text)
99. possess (HH-292, TO-268)
100. post (see text)
101. pour in (see text)
102. pour over head (see text)
103. put in (see text)
104. regularly (HH-68, TO-226)
105. shower (TO-168)
106. small (HH-473, TO-430)
107. sometimes (HH-471, TO-468)
108. stake (see text)
109. stay (HH-278, TO-647)
110. stick in ground (see text)
111. store (HH-78, TO-242)
112. taste (HH-416, TO-391)
113. tent (HH-154)
114. that (HH-351, TO-22)
115. there (TO-727)

116. think (HH-226, TO-79)
117. three (TO-p. 4)
118. tie down (see text)
119. time (HH-187, TO-595)
120. town (HH-154, TO-351)
121. true (HH-291, TO-219)
122. truly (HH-291, TO-219)
123. twice (HH-471)
124. two (TO-p. 4)
125. two weeks (HH-326)
126. use (HH-205, TO-626)
127. very (HH-473, TO-313)
128. want (HH-448, TO-173)
129. warm (HH-356, TO-137)
130. water (HH-405, TO-444)
131. week (HH-326, TO-462)
132. where (HH-183, TO-28)
133. who (HH-369, TO-12)
134. why (HH-8, TO-16)
135. wife (HH-500 + 248, TO-410)
136. with (HH-476, TO-20)
137. wow (HH-81)
138. wrap around (see text)
139. you (HH-403, TO-3)

EXERCISES

Sign the following sentences and provide an English translation.

1. Me go store; want buy chicken; want freeze; store bare.
2. House small; children many; must move. Need house big, comfortable.
3. Husband wife accompany ocean. Stay two weeks. Children leave with neighbor. Why not? That true vacation.
4. Near ocean, day hot. Night opposite; night comfortable.
5. You think crab cheap? Not. Wow! Go store, buy, true expensive.
6. Children in city must careful; car many; must look.
7. Most time me clean house regularly, keep nice; sometimes let.
8. Sometimes me drive town, sometimes change, wife drive.
9. Near town there food store, big, nice. Get food there, me enjoy.
10. Me ago live large city. Now opposite, plain.

Lesson Seven

ENGLISH ORIGINAL

Thanksgiving Dinner

I still remember our last Thanksgiving dinner. It was a real feast. Besides the turkey and dressing, we had creamed onions and green beans with almonds, a tossed salad with blue cheese dressing, sweet potatoes and giblet gravy, cranberry relish, and, for dessert, apple or pumpkin pie. The grown-ups had wine with the meal, and the children had milk. We even had home made bread with home made jelly and real butter. What made the dinner especially memorable was that we had a foreign student from South America as our guest. She was from Aruba, a small island off the coast of Venezuela. She brought a photograph album along, and after dinner we took our coffee to the living room and looked at the pictures. We thoroughly enjoyed her company. Good food and good companionship—what better combination is there?

SIGN LANGUAGE GLOSS

Thanksgiving Dinner

Past Thanksgiving dinner still remember. True feast. Have turkey, stuffing. Onion with pour-over white pour-over made from cream. And green B-E-A-N-S sprinkle A-L-M-O-N-D-S. Toss S-A-L-A-D with blue cheese spoon-on. Sweet potatoes with G-I-B-L-E-T gravy. C-R-A-N-B-E-R-R-Y R-E-L-I-S-H, and for dessert, pie, which? apple pumpkin. Adults drink wine with eat, children milk. Also bread make myself and jelly also make myself and real butter. Especially remember why? We invite girl student her home far-away, South America. Girl from A-R-U-B-A, that place small island near V-E-N-E-Z-U-E-L-A. Girl bring picture book. Eat, finish, bring coffee to living room and look-at picture. True enjoy. Good eat and good associate, join with, join, wonderful!

Past The temporal frame of reference is often established at the beginning of a statement in American Sign Language. The present text requires a past marker. Once the past marker is executed, all of the subsequent verbs are construed as past tense, whether or not they are inflected further. The citation form of the past marker moves the right hand, palm facing backward, over the right shoulder. This sign makes use of a conventional spatial domain relative to the signer which establishes everything back over the shoulder as past and everything forward from the shoulder as future. Since the present context implies that it is the immediately preceding Thanksgiving holiday that is being referenced, the sign may be modulated slightly by keeping the palm facing forward instead of turning the palm backward, and by brushing the thumb of the right hand backward along the right cheek two or three times instead of moving it back over the shoulder once. Since not all of the space toward the back over the shoulder is being used, the implication is that the time is not as far in the past as it might be; instead, it is something in the relatively recent past that is about to be discussed. In contrast, if a Thanksgiving dinner long, long ago were about to be discussed, both hands might be used and moved back over the right shoulder alternately several times, with each alternation reaching farther back over the shoulder and, thus, into the past. Additionally, to indicate the recent past, the signer might maintain eye contact with his receiver, but to indicate the remote past, the signer might break eye contact and stare off into the distance as if imagining something that took place long ago.

Thanksgiving The right "K" hand is touched to the chin and chest. This sign also means *turkey*. An abbreviated version is sometimes seen in which the right "K" hand is simply touched to the chin two or three times. Interestingly, when a sign involving considerable movement is ab-

breviated, the smaller movement that results is often repeated. For example, in the previous sign, *past,* the smaller movement backward may be compensated for by repeating the briefer movement twice. Such compensation may be necessary to make up for the loss of distinctiveness that may occur when a longer movement is abbreviated.

dinner The fingertips of the right "AND" hand are touched to the mouth several times. This is the same sign that is used for the verb, *eat.*

still The right "Y" hand is thrust straight out in front of the body, palm down. Usually the forward movement of this sign proceeds only a few inches. Prolonging the movement has the same effect as raising the pitch of the voice. It emphasizes the adverb. The sign is the same as is used for *stay, remain.* The citation form uses both "Y" hands.

remember The citation form of this sign touches the right index finger to the forehead and then presses the right thumb on the left thumb nail as both hands move forward, palms down, in front of the body. The sign is a compound, *think + remain.* An alternate version touches the right thumb to the forehead and then adds the second

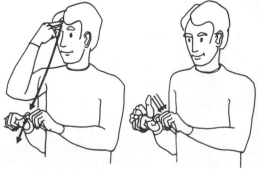

FIG. **31.** *The loss of a longer movement, as in the deletion of the first element of the compound,* **remember,** *generally requires repetition of any remaining movement or the addition of a substitute movement.*

member of the compound. An abbreviated version skips the touch of the forehead entirely and merely taps the right thumb on the left thumb nail repeatedly. This is another instance of repetition substituting for a loss of a larger movement (see Fig. 31).

True The right index finger, pointing upward, is touched to the lips and then moved forward somewhat emphatically. The force of the forward movement may be varied so as to express various degrees of emphasis.

feast The sign for *eat* or *dinner* may be modified by alternating the movements with both hands and repeating them for several times. This is the second instance in which an alternating movement repeated several times has the effect of emphasizing the basic concept. The previous instance was *long-ago*, using both hands alternately over the right shoulder. Here, signing *eat, eat, eat* alternately with both hands inplies a lot of eating, and, therefore, a *feast*. Additionally, instead of merely bringing the fingertips to the lips, the movement may be enlarged by executing circles toward the mouth which proceed down the throat before the hands return to their initial position and repeat the movement.

Have The fingertips of both hands are touched to the chest. Since the past tense has already been established by the previous marker, all of the verbs are construed as past even though they are uninflected. The appropriate English translation of this text would put the verbs in the past.

turkey This is the same sign as was indicated previously for *Thanksgiving*.

stuffing The left "C" hand is held, palm down, so that the arch of the hand represents the carcass of the turkey. The right "AND" hand is then shoved repeatedly into the cavity formed by the left "C" hand so as to imitate the act of stuffing the bird. Such improvisation is found frequently in American Sign Language for communicating when conventional signs are not in general use.

onion The knuckle of the right "X" hand is touched to the corner of the right eye and

twisted. This sign is probably motivated by the tears that onions sometimes cause. A plural marker is unnecessary, since the context plainly implies a collective, *onions*.

with The knuckles of both "A" hands touch as the "A" hands are placed together in front of the body. The same sign may also mean *together*. If both "A" hands in the *with* position are moved forward from the body, the sign becomes a verb, *accompany*. The opposite, *without*, forms the sign for *with* as the initial position, and then both hands open as they are dropped apart, as if discarding their contents.

pour-over This is also an improvisation. There is no conventional sign for cream sauce. But if one acts out pouring something over the onions and then adds some explanation for the pouring, it is likely that the notion of some kind of sauce will be understood. The sign can be made by using the right fist to represent the container with the thumb extended for a spout. The pouring action should hover over a small area, as if confined to a vegetable bowl of onions.

white pour-over The fingertips and thumb of the right hand brush against the front of the body as the hand is drawn forward, ending with the fingers touching in the "AND" configuration. The sign may be derived from grasping a white shirt front to indicate the color. In a similar fashion, the color *red* is indicated by touching the lips with the right index finger, and *black* is indicated by stroking the right eyebrow with the side of the right index finger. All three of these colors are indicated by touching a part of the body where an example of the color may be found. The pouring activity is repeated to make it clear that the white is a description of what is being poured over the onions. The signer may emphasize the explanatory nature of this information by maintaining direct eye contact with his receiver.

make The fists or "S" hands are twisted back and forth at the wrists while they are bumped together several times in front of the body, the one on top of the other. An alternate version simply rubs the fists or

"S" hands together as the wrists twist them back and forth several times.

from The left index finger is extended as a point of reference, and the curved right index finger is drawn toward the body and away from the left index finger. This is a typical strategy in American Sign Language for indicating prepositions. The left hand provides a point of reference, and the meaning of the preposition is indicated by the position or the movement of the right hand relative to the left. The sign may be executed with a twist of the wrist that raises the curved index finger up in the air as the right hand is drawn toward the body.

cream The right "C" hand scrapes over the opening of the left "0" hand or over the back of the left hand as if scraping cream off of the surface of some milk. Again, since this is explanatory, the signer may maintain eye contact with the receiver so as to insure his attention to the explanation and to set it off from the rest of the narrative. Recalling the menu may be done with eye contact broken, as the signer stares off into the distance so as to re-live the experience. His facial expression may also add to the effect by suggesting a dreamy or reminiscent attitude as each dish from the dinner is recalled in turn.

And The conjunction, *and,* is rarely used in American Sign Language. Typically, a pause establishes a connection between coordinate clauses, phrases, or words. Occasionally the conjunction, *and,* may be used for emphasis. The sign seems to take what is given on the left and draw it across the front of the body so as to link it up with what is on the right.

green The right "G" hand is shaken with twists of the wrist in front of the body. Several other colors are made similarly: *yellow* with the "Y" hand, *purple* with the "P" hand, and *blue* with the "B" hand.

B-E-A-N-S The capitals in the gloss and the caps with hyphens in the notes suggest that this word be fingerspelled. There is a sign that might be used: the right thumb and index finger are pinched together to indicate something small, and they are touched to the edge of the extended left index finger, sometimes moving toward the tip. In an alternate version they pinch the tip of the left index finger. But this same sign may also mean *pea, seed, cherry,* or anything else that is small. In the present text, *green* plus the sign for *seed* or *small fruit* might be misconstrued as *pea.* To avoid such ambiguity, it is suggested that the item be fingerspelled. This is not meant to suggest that American Sign Language is deficient as a language because it lacks unambiguous symbols for various fruits and vegetables. The ready availability of vocabulary from English to supplement the vocabulary of signs has made it relatively unnecessary for deaf people to develop signs for all of the referents that they might wish to name. There are no signs for the months of the year, for various makes of cars, for brand names of merchandise, and other items which are likely to be referenced frequently.

sprinkle Again, a bit of pantomime may be invoked here. The right hand may be held with the fingers together and pointed downward over the imaginary bowl of green beans, and the fingers may be rubbed together as the hand moves over the imaginary bowl, as if something is being sprinkled on the contents.

A-L-M-O-N-D-S There is no conventional sign for *almonds;* it will have to be fingerspelled.

Toss S-A-L-A-D Both hands may be used to *toss* an imaginary salad, holding imaginary spoons. It is a common recourse in American Sign Language to involve imaginary objects as part of the execution of a sign. Previously in the present text, imaginary bowls of vegetables were localized in front of the signer so as to make it appropriate to pour or sprinkle something over the vegetables. The freedom to invoke imaginary objects greatly enhances the scope of pantomime as a vehicle for communicating. In the present case, the long-handled salad tools must be held in the same way as one would hold such implements in their actual use. The tossing action would be done carefully, without much wrist activity, since careless tossing merely spills the salad. *S-A-L-A-D* is fingerspelled.

with blue cheese *With* and *blue* are signed as indicated previously. *Cheese* is signed by pressing the palms of both hands together in front of the body and then rubbing them as the wrists are twisted in opposite directions. One twist may suffice, or several smaller twists may be executed.

spoon-on The right "H" hand, representing a spoon, acts out the spooning of dressing on to the salad, which is now localized on the table in front of the signer. Notice that overt localization strategies are not required for objects which tend to have a natural location relative to the signer. Since a salad is likely to be served directly in front of a person at a table, that location may be used for subsequent referencing. As with the tossing of the salad, the movements associated with *spooning* the dressing on the salad should match rather closely the movements ordinarily required for such an activity.

sweet The fingertips of the right "H" hand stroke the lips one or more times. If the action is done once, it may be executed more slowly and deliberately, pausing over the lips briefly. If it is repeated, it may be executed with less downward movement, with the knuckles merely bending repeatedly so as to touch the lips with a slightly downward movement several times. The sign is also used metaphorically for *cute*. A variant uses the fingertips of the entire right hand brushed downward on the lips one or more times. The same signs may mean *candy* or *sugar*.

potatoes The curved right "V" hand, representing a fork, is stabbed against the back of the left fist. Since the expression *sweet potatoes* is a compound, it is likely that the first portion of the sign, *sweet*, will be abbreviated somewhat. This would argue for a single downward movement over the lips for the first portion of the sign, with the second portion prolonged by touching the left fist twice with the right curved "V" hand.

with G-I-B-L-E-T gravy *With* is signed as indicated previously. *G-I-B-L-E-T* is fin-

gerspelled. *Gravy* is signed by holding the left hand, palm facing right, in front of the body, and the thumb and index finger of the right hand grasp the fleshy portion of the left hand that is toward the bottom and scrape off of it several times. The sign may suggest gravy dripping from a piece of meat.

C-R-A-N-B-E-R-R-Y R-E-L-I-S-H Both of these words would probably be fingerspelled. Students of American Sign Language should be advised to fingerspell as smoothly as possible. Speed is less important than rhythm. The hand should be held in a relaxed position, and unnecessary movements should be avoided. The hand should move gracefully from one letter position to the next without jerking the hand forward or bouncing it around as each letter is executed. Double letters are indicated either by touching the fingers together twice, as in R-R, or by moving the hand slightly to the right, as in C-C or L-L.

and for dessert *And* is signed as indicated previously. *For* touches the right index fingertip to the forehead and then turns the tip outward as the finger is hooked forward from the forehead. It has been suggested that this sign was invented by the Abbe de L'Epee to translate the French *pour*, which expresses purpose. *Dessert* may be signed by touching the two "D" hands together in front of the body or by touching the right "D" hand to the lips in the same location where *sweet* is signed. The latter sign may need support from the context to distinguish it from *dentist,* which is also signed by touching the right "D" hand to the mouth.

pie The sign for *pie* is made by using the left palm to represent a pie, and the edge of the right hand, representing a knife, cuts the left palm into four pieces.

which? Both "A" hands are held, thumbs pointing up, in front of the body, and they are raised alternately up and down in an ambivalent manner. Since the sign is a question, the signer may establish eye contact with the receiver, pretending for the moment that the receiver is at the dinner and has a choice, and ask *which?* Or the signer may look at each hand in turn as it is raised up in front of him as if he, himself, were deliberating over the choice.

apple The thumb of the right "A" hand is touched to the right cheek, and the hand is then rocked forward several times with twists of the wrist. An alternate version uses the knuckle of the right "X" hand to execute the sign.

pumpkin The left hand is balled into a fist to represent a melon, and the right hand snaps the middle finger against the back of the melon as if testing it to see if it sounds ripe. The same sign also means *watermelon,* but the context here makes it unambiguous. Following the signs for *apple* and *pumpkin* the signer may pause, holding his hands in a natural gesture as if waiting for a choice to be made.

Adults The sign for *tall* is used here: the bent "B" hand is elevated above the head as if to indicate a person tall in stature. If the sign is repeated alternately with both hands, the sign takes on the meaning *adults* or *grown-ups.*

drink The right hand forms a "C," representing a cup, and the sign is executed by taking an imaginary drink from the right "C" hand. If just the thumb and index finger hold an imaginary cocktail glass, the sign *drink* may refer to a stronger intoxicating beverage.

wine A "W" on the right hand makes a small circle near the right cheek.

with eat Both of these signs are executed as indicated previously. *Eat* can serve as either a noun, *food* or *meal,* or as a verb, *eat, dine.*

children The two hands, palms down, pat imaginary children on the head as the hands move sideways apart from one another. One hand may be used instead of two. The hands may indicate decreasing stature as they move out toward the sides.

milk The right fist is squeezed together several times in a gesture vaguely resembling milking a cow.

Also The sign for *same, also* may be executed deliberately with a somewhat larger movement than usual for emphasis. The index fingers pointing forward are placed next to each other slightly to the left in front of the body, and then they are placed next to each other again slightly to the right in front of the body. An alternate sign for *also same, similarly* is executed with the right "Y" hand, palm down, placed first in one location and then in another in front of the body so as to establish the similarity or sameness of the things being compared.

bread The left hand is held, palm toward the body, in a bent "B" configuration, and the fingertips of the right bent "B" hand make slicing motions from the left fingertips down toward the knuckles. The sign imitates the European manner of slicing bread, holding the loaf under the left arm and slicing with a knife held in the right hand. In the present sign, the right hand represents the knife while the left arm holds the imaginary loaf.

make myself *Make* is signed as indicated previously. *Myself* uses a hand configuration that is used for all reflexives, the right "A" hand, thumb up. In this case, the back of the thumb is pressed two or three times against the chest of the signer. For *ourselves* the same hand configuration is touched to the signer's right and then the left shoulder. *Yourself* is directed toward the receiver, and *yourselves* is directed toward several imaginary or real persons, including the receiver. *Himself* and *herself* are directed off to the side toward a real or imagined referent, and *themselves* is directed toward several imaginary referents.

with jelly make myself All of the signs here have been used before except *jelly.* For *jelly* the right "J" hand is drawn in the left palm.

and real butter *And* is signed as indicated previously. Some of the "ands" that are indicated in the present gloss are expendable. The sign for *real* is the same as the sign for *true,* except here the right index finger may first be rubbed upward against the lips before moving forward from the face in order to add emphasis. *Butter* is signed by rubbing the fingertips of the right "H" hand in the left palm several times, brushing them toward the body as if scraping butter off the palm with a knife.

Especially The left index finger is pointed upward, and the right thumb and index finger grasp it by the tip and pull it upward in front of the body. This same sign in other contexts may mean *except, exceptional.*

remember why? The sign for remember is executed as indicated previously. *Why?* is signed by holding the right "B" hand with the palm facing the right side of the forehead, the fingertips of the index, middle, and fourth fingers are brushed against the forehead as the hand is dipped downward and then brought forward from the forehead, ending in a "Y" configuration. This is a typical strategy in American Sign Language for indicating a reason. In English this would ordinarily be expressed with a causal clause: "I especially remember it because we invited a student etc." In American Sign Language the causal clause is introduced by posing an interrogative, *Why?* as if that were the question that naturally would occur to the receiver. Then the explanation is given. A slight pause might follow the *Why?* Also, a questioning facial expression together with eye contact with the receiver might assist in establishing the rapport that is implied by putting the question in the mind of the receiver.

We The right index finger is touched to the right and to the left shoulder. This sign may be initialized by executing it with the right "W" touched to the same locations (see Fig. 32). Initialized signs such as this were introduced to American Sign Language by educators who were desirous of more agreement between signs and English words. By retaining the location, movement, and hand orientation of the original sign from the American Sign Language, it was expected that the meaning associated with the sign would not be lost by changing the hand configuration. The hand configuration was changed so as to agree with the first letter of the cognate English word. This effort to modify American Sign Language in the hope of making it more compatible with English has gone on for quite some time, and there are a large number of initialized signs in the lexicon. Previous examples in the present text are the colors, *blue, green, yellow,* and *purple,* and the signs for *wine, dessert,* and *jelly.* Initialized signs are complex symbols for which there is no counterpart in any spoken language. While the basic location, movement, and hand orientation refer to the field of meaning that is associated with a conventional sign from the lexicon, the hand configuration references a related English word. Whether deaf persons customarily think of the English word as such signs are executed is another matter. It seems likely that young deaf children growing up and leaning American Sign Language from models in their environment may gradually acquire a feel for the meaning of signs such as these without even knowing that there is an English word beginning with the indicated letter that means more or less the same thing. The "more or less" is an important qualification, since the field of meaning associated with a particular sign may differ considerably from the field of meaning associated with a related English word.

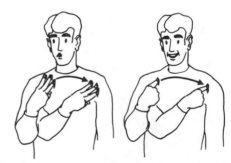

FIG. 32. *Initialized signs reference the field of meaning associated with a conventional sign, and by means of the hand configuration they also reference an English cognate.*

invite This is a compound sign. The fingertips of the right hand are struck lightly on the back of the left fist, a sign that is ordinarily associated with calling someone to attention, and then the right bent "B" hand, palm up, makes a sweeping gesture from a point distant from the body toward the signer, as if welcoming someone with a friendly gesture.

girl The thumb of the right "A" hand is brushed downward along the right jaw or cheek. This sign is said to have been derived from a gender marker developed by de l'Epee to indicate the difference between male and female genders in French. The male gender marker was based on the custom of tipping a hat, and the region of the forehead serves as the gender marker for male kinship signs. The female gender marker was derived from the bonnet strings tied under the chin. Much of the original movement has been lost, but the hand configuration appropriate for holding a bonnet string and the region of the cheek have survived. Thus, the region of the right cheek serves as a gender marker for female kinship signs. These gender markers may also be used to indicate the gender of persons who are not related, as in the present case. The student is described as female by executing the sign which constitutes the female gender marker.

student The sign for *student* is derived from the sign for *learn:* The right hand is brought down toward the left palm, and the thumb and fingers are brought together as the hand reaches the palm as if taking something from it and then bringing it to the head. *Student* is a compound of *learn + the person marker.* The person marker is executed by drawing both hands, palms toward the body, downward along the sides of the body. This same marker may be added to nouns (*farm + person marker = farmer*) or verbs (*teach + person marker = teacher*). That it is not a one-to-one equivalent for the English suffix, *-er,* is plain from the present example, since *student* not only does not use the *-er* suffix but it is derived from *study* rather than *learn* (see Fig. 33). When compounds are formed in American Sign Language, the first component of the sign is often abbreviated. In the present example, the sign for *learn* would not be executed with the right hand going all the way up to the forehead. In executing the compound sign, *student,* after the right hand takes the imaginary material to be learned from the left palm, it would join with the other hand in the execution of the person marker without being raised much higher than the waist.

her Possession is indicated in American Sign Language by the open palm directed toward the noun or pronoun to which the possessive marker is to be attached. In this case, the female student is imagined to be located in front of the signer, and the open palm is directed outward toward the imaginary student.

home The fingertips of the right "AND" hand are touched to the lips and to the cheek. In an alternate version it is the flat

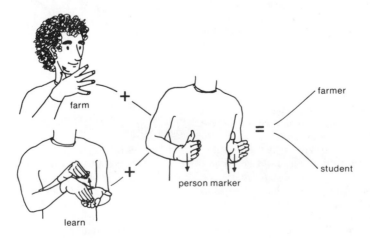

FIG. 33. *The person marker is comparable but not identical to the English suffix,* **-er.**

hand that is touched to the cheek. The sign is said to be derived from the notion of home being a place to eat and sleep.

far-away The left "A" hand, thumb up, is held in front of the body, and the right "A" hand, thumb up, is moved from an initial position near the left hand to a point far from the left hand and outward from the body. If the signer frowns while signing *far-away,* the emphasis changes the meaning to *very far away.* In an alternate version of the sign the right hand is used without the left. Many signs may be executed one-handed without loss of clarity or change of meaning. Apparently there is enough redundancy in American Sign Language gestures that one can hold an object in the left hand and sign with the right hand, only, and the receiver will be able to supply the missing contribution that would ordinarily be made by the left hand. Sometimes the one-handed version of a sign may be somewhat less formal than the two-handed version.

South America The points of the compass are initialized signs moved off in four different directions. Which direction is established as north is arbitrary, but once north is established, the other directions are ordinarily indicated appropriately relative to the established direction of *north.* If *north* and *south* are the only directions at stake, *north* may be signed by moving the right "N" hand upward, and *south* may be signed by moving the right "S" hand downward. If *north* and *south* are signed by moving the right "N" or "S" hand forward and backward, respectively, then *east* and *west* are signed by moving the right "E" and "W" hand, respectively, right and left. The relation of these signs to the points of the compasss is illustrated in Figure 34. *America* is signed by interlacing the fingers of both hands and then moving the interlocked hands in a horizontal counterclockwise circle in front of the body. The sign for *America* is said to be derived from a split rail fence.

Girl The female gender marker may be followed by a sign indicating stature for *girl.* In this way one can indicate a very *young girl* by signing *female + short* and a girl who is grown up by signing *female + tall.*

from A-R-U-B-A *From* is signed as indicated previously. *A-R-U-B-A* is fingerspelled.

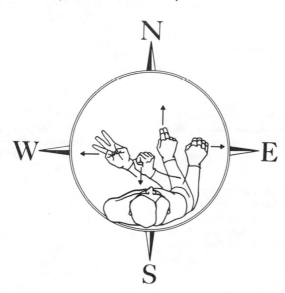

FIG. 34. *The directions, North, South, East, and West, correspond to the points of an imaginary compass.*

that The right "Y" hand, palm down, is struck into the palm of the left hand. In this case, Aruba is far away, and the sign for *that* may be executed with the palm of the right "Y" hand directed off in the distance. As an alternative, the sign *that* may be signed with the left hand and aimed at the right hand, which has just spelled *A-R-U-B-A.*

place Both "P" hands trace a small area or *place* in a horizontal plane in front of the body.

small island *Small* is indicated by moving the palms of both hands toward each other in front of the body as if indicating a small amount or a small area. The sign for *place* may be executed with the smallness in mind. A smaller area than usual may be marked off, and the sign for *small* may be executed directly over the area indicated by the sign for *place. Island* may be signed by tracing a small circle on the back of the left fist with the right "I" hand.

near The bent left "B" hand, palm toward the body, is held in front of the body so as to provide a point of reference, and the right hand is brought toward and almost in contact with the left hand. The direction of movement may be either from close to the body toward the left hand, with the back of the right bent "B" hand approaching the palm of the left, or from out from the body toward the left hand, with the palm of the right bent "B" hand approaching the back of the left. In the present case, since Venezuela is rather far away from the United States, it might be appropriate to have the direction of movement go away from the body toward the left hand.

V-E-N-E-Z-U-E-L-A The name of the country is fingerspelled.

Girl bring *Girl* is signed as indicated previously. *Bring* is signed by holding both hands, palms up, about shoulder high off to the right from the body and then bringing them laterally toward the midline, keeping the palms up. The same sign also means *carry, serve.* Followed by the *person marker* it means *waiter, servant.*

picture book For *picture*, the left hand is held with the palm toward the face, and the right "C" hand is placed against the palm one or more times. In an alternate version the palm of the left hand is turned outward, and the index finger edge of the right "C" hand is touched to the palm one or more times. Since these are pictures that are going to be looked at as in a book, it is likely that the first version of the sign would be used. It also allows for an easy transition to *book:* the hands are held with the palms pressed together and then opened as if they were the covers of a book.

Eat finish *Eat* is signed the same as *dinner. Finish* is used very frequently in American Sign Language to indicate an action completed in the past. In this case, the sequence of the signs implies a temporal sequence of the actions, "When we had finished eating," or "after we had finished eating." The sign for *finish* is executed by holding one or both hands, palms turned slightly upward with the fingers spread apart, and then turning them over quickly with a twist of the wrist. The sign may also mean *done, over with.* As an imperative it can mean either *get it over with* or, as an interesting twist, *stop that.*

bring coffee *Bring* is signed as indicated previously, except that here the motion begins in front of the body and moves off to the side, in the direction of the imaginary living room. For *coffee*, the left fist represents an old-fashioned coffee grinder, and the right hand turns the imaginary crank counterclockwise over the left fist.

to living-room Like other prepositions, *to* uses the left hand as a point of reference, and the meaning is derived from the movement or the relation of the right hand relative to the left. In this case the left index finger is extended, and the tip of the right index finger is touched to the tip of the left. Living room may be signed as a compound derived from English: *live* + *room. Live* is signed by drawing both "A" hands or both "L" hands up the chest. *Room* is signed by marking off a square in a horizontal plane using both "R" hands. The "R" hands may either trace the area or they may indicate opposite walls in turn by extending them horizontally. Another way to indicate *living-room* is by touching the thumb of the right "5" hand to the chest two or three times. This is the sign for *fine*, and the room in the house that is *fine* is the *living-room*.

and look-at picture *And* is signed as indicated previously. *Look-at* uses the right "V" hand. The fingertips of the right "V" hand are first directed toward the eyes in the initial position, and then turned out so as to be directed at the object of the signer's gaze. In this case the picture book is likely to be imagined as located directly in front of him, and he can move the right "V" hand in a scanning motion similar to the sign for *read*. *Picture* is signed as indicated previously. To pluralize the noun, the left palm may be moved from left to right in front of the face as the right "C" hand is placed against it several times. After the sign for *picture* establishes a location for them against the left palm, the sign for *read, look-at,* may be repeated, using the left palm as the spatial reference for what is looked at.

True enjoy True is signed as indicated previously. For *enjoy* the palms of both hands are rubbed on the stomach and chest. The right hand is generally above the left, although this is not mandatory.

Good eat The sign for *good* touches the tips of the fingers of the right hand to the lips and then drops the back of the hand down into the upturned left palm. The right hand may be used without the left.

And good associate *Associate* uses both "A" hands with the thumb of the left hand

pointing up and the thumb of the right hand pointing down. The thumbs circle one another in a horizontal plane several times. This same sign may also translate the English pronoun, *one another*.

join the circular portions of both "F" hands are linked together by joining them in front of the body.

with Both fists are placed side by side, fingers touching, in front of the body.

join *Join* is repeated again for emphasis.

Wonderful The right "F" hand is brought forward from the face and to an abrupt stop with a smug facial expression. This may serve as a natural gesture among hearing persons. The ease with which such natural gestures can be assimilated by a Sign Language message calls attention to the ease with which deaf persons draw on a wide range of available resources as they communicate manually. They do not limit themselves to conventional signs from the American Sign Language, but they also make use of fingerspelling, pantomime, and natural, expressive gestures. Some of these expressive gestures may also become somewhat conventional among hearing persons, as in the present case. Almost all hearing persons in our society would recognize the "F" hand brought forward and stopped abruptly as a sign of pleasure and approval. There is also a conventional sign for *wonderful* in American Sign Language, in which the palms of both hands are presented forward and outward from the body.

VOCABULARY

1. accompany (HH-476, TO-19)
2. adults (HH-244)
3. almonds (fingerspell)
4. also (HH-452, TO-104)
5. America (HH-485, TO-166)
6. and (HH-46, TO-239)
7. apple (HH-264)
8. Aruba (fingerspell)
9. associate (HH-185, TO-122)
10. beans (fingerspell)
11. black (HH-284, TO-88)
12. blue (HH-353, TO-437)
13. book (HH-237, TO-181)
14. bread (HH-56, TO-263)
15. bring (HH-91, TO-52)
16. bring together (see text)
17. butter (TO-616)
18. candy (HH92, TO-256)
19. carry (HH-91, TO-52)
20. cheese (HH-477)
21. cherry (see text)
22. children (HH-40, TO-147)
23. coffee (HH-128, TO-297)
24. cranberry (fingerspell)
25. cream (HH-265, TO-493)
26. cute (HH-92, TO-256)
27. dentist (see text)
28. dessert (see text)
29. dine (HH-491, TO-235)
30. dinner (HH-491, TO-235)
31. done (HH-214, TO-174)
32. drink (TO-403)
33. eat (HH-491, TO-235)
34. enjoy (HH-42, TO-255)
35. especially (HH-330, TO-554)
36. except (HH-330, TO-554)
37. exceptional (HH-330, TO-554)
38. far away (HH-340)
39. feast (HH-491, TO-235)
40. female (HH-500, TO-106)
41. fine (HH-444, TO-135)
42. finish (HH-214, TO-174)
43. food (HH-491, TO-235)
44. for (HH-404, TO-18)
45. from (HH-16, TO-33)
46. giblet (fingerspell)
47. girl (HH-500, TO-106)
48. good (HH-342, TO-259)
49. gravy (HH-439, TO-497)
50. green (HH-353, TO-434)
51. have (HH-292, TO-268)
52. her (HH-469)
53. herself (HH-119)
54. himself (HH-119)
55. home (HH-489, TO-241)
56. invite (HH-261, TO-355)
57. island (see text)
58. jelly (see text)
59. join (HH-33, TO-543)
60. law (HH-287, TO-522)
61. lawyer (HH-287 + 18)
62. learn (HH-217, TO-579)
63. live (HH-446, TO-119)
64. living room (HH-444, TO-135)
65. long ago (HH-118, TO-205)
66. look at (HH-413, TO-209)
67. make (HH-210, TO-298)
68. meal (HH-491, TO-235)
69. milk (HH-265, TO-479)
70. myself (HH-87, TO-9)
71. near (HH-163, TO-367)
72. north (HH-161, TO-474)
73. onion (see text)
74. ourselves (HH-119, TO-11)
75. over with (HH-214, TO-174)
76. past (HH-118, TO-205)
77. pea (see text)
78. person (HH-18, TO-426)
79. picture (HH-115, TO-488)
80. pie (HH-56)
81. place (HH-44, TO-433)
82. potato (HH-329, TO-601)
83. pour over (see text)
84. pumpkin (see text)
85. purple (HH-353, TO-439)
86. read (HH-208, TO-585)
87. real (HH-291, TO-219)
88. red (HH-425, TO-436)
89. relish (fingerspell)
90. remain (HH-278, TO-647)

91. remember (HH-226, TO-118)
92. room (TO-358)
93. salad (fingerspell)
94. same (HH-452, TO-104)
95. servant (HH-91 + 18)
96. serve (HH-91)
97. seed (see text)
98. similarly (see text)
99. small (HH-473, TO-430)
100. South (HH-161, TO-474)
101. South America (HH-161 + 485, TO-474 + 166)
102. spoon on (see text)
103. sprinkle (see text)
104. stay (HH-278, TO-647)
105. still (HH-278, TO-647)
106. stop that (HH-214, TO-174)
107. student (HH-217 + 18, TO-579)
108. stuffing (see text)
109. sugar (HH-92, TO-256)
110. sweet (HH-92, TO-257)
111. tall (HH-244, TO-473)
112. teach (HH-123, TO-253)
113. teacher (HH-123 + 18)

114. Thanksgiving (see text)
115. that (HH-351, TO-22)
116. themselves (HH-119)
117. think (HH-226, TO-79)
118. to (HH-240, TO-30)
119. together (HH-476, TO-19)
120. toss (see text)
121. true (HH-291, TO-219)
122. turkey (HH-111)
123. Venezuela (fingerspell)
124. waiter (HH-91 + 18)
125. we (HH-137, TO-4)
126. which (HH-333, TO-130)
127. white (HH-459, TO-238)
128. why (HH-8, TO-16)
129. wine (HH-437, TO-445)
130. with (HH-476, TO-20)
131. without (HH-476, TO-21)
132. wonderful (HH-140, TO-265)
133. yellow (HH-353, TO-438)
134. young girl (HH-500 + 40)
135. yourself (HH-119, TO-10)
136. yourselves (HH-119, TO-10)

EXERCISES

Sign the following sentences and provide an English translation.

1. Me enjoy look at picture.

2. Milk for children good.

3. Teacher live near have children cute.

4. Butter make from cream.

5. Bread home make with jelly home make that fine dessert.

6. You drink coffee black coffee with cream which?

7. Me remember ago me look at small island far away, green; that island true wonderful place. Still remember.

8. Wine drink with cheese, good which, white, red, which?

9. We invite lawyer dinner, himself bring dessert, pie make from sweet potato.

10. We read book have picture picture picture South American; book teach; we learn.

Lesson Eight

ENGLISH ORIGINAL

A Shopping Expedition

Last week I took my son, David, into town to buy him a new pair of shoes. His feet seem to have grown an inch in the past month, and he was complaining that his shoes hurt his feet. It took me the better part of the afternoon to find something I could afford. The first store I went in had nothing under $10.00. The second store had some cheap shoes, but they were really poor. Finally, I found a pretty good pair for $6.50. I had no idea that shoes were so expensive or that good shoes were so hard to find at a reasonable price. Now I'm afraid to think about buying him new clothes. I can just see $8.00 shirts and a $45.00 coat coming up. You know what will happen. David will get the new clothes, and I will be left with last year's. I think I will gain 10 pounds. Then I can say I grew, too, and that I also need new clothes.

SIGN LANGUAGE GLOSS

Travel Shop

Week + ago take my son David (D) downtown. What-for? Buy new shoes. Since past month his feet seem big inch. He complain, complain, complain old shoes hurt feet. Almost all afternoon use-up before succeed. Buy shoes can afford. First store go-in, nothing below $10.00. Second store have cheap shoes few. Poor, no-good. Later succeed, find shoes worth $6.50. Shoes true expensive; me idea no. Me expect look-around can find shoes good cheap. Me wrong. Must search, search, hard. Terrible. Think Clothes. Will need new. Think! Me afraid think. Can foresee future, shirt $8. Coat $45. Happen? Know you. (D) will get new clothes; me same last-year. Maybe me gain 10 pounds. Then can say me grow " " also need new clothes.

GRAMMATICAL NOTES

Week +ago The temporal frame of reference for this narrative is established at the outset as a week ago. The sign for *week* is inflected by the addition of a past marker. Ordinarily the past marker throws the left palm over the right shoulder, but if the sign for week is followed by the same movement but with the hand configuration retaining the extended index finger of the sign for *week*, the meaning is made explicit as *last week*. If the right index finger is moved forward from the body with a flourish, the sign means *next week*. The past and future modulations of *week* are illustrated in Figure 35.

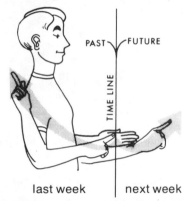

last week   next week

FIG. 35. *The movement of the right hand may constitute a time marker, forward for the future* **(next week)** *and backward for the past* **(last week).**

take There is no citation form of *take* listed in most conventional American Sign Language dictionaries. Perhaps the reason for this is that the sign for *take* is ordinarily modified so as to take into account what it is that is being taken. In this case, one might imagine that the son is at the right side where one can *take* him by the arm and drag him forward as if to lead him on a shopping trip. As an alternative, one might use the sign for *bring, carry:* one or both hands, palms up, are moved from right to left at about shoulder height.

my son The possessive marker in American Sign Language is the open palm. Placed

against the signer's chest, the sign means *my*. Directed elsewhere it may mean *your* (singular or plural, depending on whether the hand is directed toward a single person, real or imaginary, or swept across a group), *his, her, hers, their* or *theirs* (see Fig. 36). *Son* is a compound, *male + baby*. The male gender marker is also used with compounds meaning *husband (male + marry)* and *brother (Male + same).*

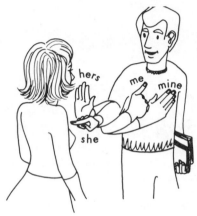

FIG. 36. *The open palm is the possessive marker in American Sign Language.*

David Proper names may be fingerspelled, but members of a family and close friends and associates generally know one another's name signs. A name sign is typically an initialized sign, using the first letter of the person's first name, although this is not always the case. Some name signs are nicknames, but they are generally not derogatory. In this case, *David* needs a name sign. Our choice is somewhat arbitrary and not very original—we suggest a "D" tapped on the left shoulder.

downtown The fingertips of both hands may be tapped together a few times in front of the chest. This sign resembles the sign for *city*. Out of context, it may be impossible to distinguish them. There is another sign that may be used for *downtown:* The right "M" hand makes a circle above the left palm and then is brought downward so as to touch the middle of the left palm with the fingertips of the right "M" hand. This sign also means *middle, center,* and undoubtedly derives the meaning *downtown* from the fact that downtown areas are typically in the middle of a city.

What-for Instead of a cumbersome purpose clause, the signer may put the question in the receiver's mind as to why he or she was taking David downtown. The question, *What-for* occurs relatively frequently in informal conversation in American Sign Language. It is derived from the sign for *for,* the right index finger touched with the fingertip to the forehead and then brought forward so that the palm faces outward in front of the forehead. This sign is often used as a preposition, and its meaning typically has something to do with purpose or intent. The question is marked with an appropriate facial expression-raised eyebrows, final position of the sign held expectantly, and direct eye contact with the receiver. The direct eye contact is especially important here, not only because it is a question but also because it is a rapport establishing question. It is the receiver who is supposed to be wondering *what* for?.

Buy The sign for *buy* is related to the sign for *money.* The right hand is held in the "AND" configuration, and the backs of the right fingers are first placed in the left palm and then moved forward toward an imaginary sales person. If the same sign is repeated several times, it means *shop, go shopping.*

new The left hand is held in front of the body, palm up, and the right hand, palm up, is brought toward the left so that the back of the right hand scrapes the left palm as the right hand moves off toward the left of the signer's body.

shoes There are several different signs for *shoes* in use around the country, probably reflecting dialect differences. Each residential school for the deaf has certain signs that are used only there and nowhere else. When the pupils from a particular school grow up and move elsewhere, they tend to retain some of the usages that were found in their school environment. In this way a regional dialect emerges, supported by the usage that is in effect at the state school.

One sign for *shoes* holds both "S" hands, palms down, in front of the body, and the sides of the fists are knocked together. Another sign holds the left "C" hand, palm up, in such a way that the right hand, palm down, can be slipped into it as if putting on a shoe or slipper. Another sign for *shoe* or *shoes* holds the left fist, palm down, in front of the body, and the knuckles of the right fist are knocked against the back of the left fist. The sign is similar to *rock, hard,* but the orientation of the hands is different. In *shoe* or *shoes* the knuckles of both hands are oriented in the same direction, while for *hard, rock,* they are not.

Since This sign is used very frequently in American Sign Language for an action that began in the past and continues until the present. It may also be used to indicate the recent passage of time. Thus, *since two weeks* may be translated "For two weeks." The sign may be derived from *happen. Happen* is signed by holding both hands, palms up, in front of the body, index fingers extended. Both hands are then turned over so that they are palms down, index fingers still extended and parallel to one another. In *since* the extended index fingers are initially placed over the right shoulder, the right hand above the left. Both hands are brought forward and downward to a final position in front of the body, and the hands turn over so as to be palms down in the final position, similar to the final position for *happen.* This conjecture regarding the relationship between *since* and *happen* is ventured partly because there is another temporal sign that also seems to be derived from *happen,* namely, *during.* Here, the two hands are moved forward from the body as they are turned over. The forward movement has the effect of tacking a future marker on the sign for *happen,* and whatever *happens* over the course of time, beginning in the present and extending into the future, can be said to happen *during* the time frame that has been established for the narrative. Of course, *during* may also be glossed as *while.* In the sign for *since,* there is also a temporal marker, this time a past marker, associated with the initial position. The movement from the past marker position to the present position establishes the meaning as extending from the past and to the present. The use of spatial domains for the purpose of expressing temporal relations and durations is an important structural feature of American Sign Language. The fact that space is continuous makes the system radically different from the way in which tenses are ordinarily used in spoken languages. But there is also a certain amount of discontinuity, and it is possible that spatial domains associated with past, present, and future times are perceived categorically. Research on the categorical perception of signs and structural features of signs is just beginning to be undertaken, and the exploration of the subtleties of the use of spatial domains to handle temporal frames of reference has only recently begun.

past month The recent past, which is one of the temporal boundaries on the sign, *since,* is indicated by the general past marker along with the sign for *month*. For *past* the right hand, palm facing backward, is moved backward over the right shoulder. The past marker may either precede or follow the sign for *month,* and it might be translated either "Last month" or "a month ago." *Month* is signed by holding the left index finger pointing upward, and the right index finger, held horizontally, scrapes down the back of the left index finger. It has been suggested that the sign is derived from the act of tearing pages off of a wall calendar.

his The possessive marker, the open palm, is used again, this time pointing off toward the left. The left localization of David is somewhat arbitrary, but since his name sign is executed on the left shoulder, the left side of the signer's body is a convenient place to imagine that David is located for pronominal referencing. If there is any ambiguity suspected, the name sign, (D) may precede the possessive marker, *Last month (D) his.*

feet The right index finger is pointed downward at the signer's feet. The double downward movement makes the sign relatively unambiguous.

seem The right hand is held so that the palm is turned toward the face at the side of the head. The hand is then turned slowly with a twist of the wrist so that the final position finds the hand in front of the face with the palm toward the eyes.

big The two "L" hands with the thumb and index finger curled into hooks are held, palms facing, in front of the chest. They are brought apart to the sides with a jerk. A similar movement in the same location is used for *much* (open hands), *very* ("V" hands) and *large* ("L" hands).

inch This is a natural gesture. The right hand indicates an inch by presenting the thumb and index finger with a gap between in a horizontal plane. *Seem big inch* would be translated either "They seem to have grown an inch" or "they seem bigger by an inch."

He Here the usefulness of localizing David at the side of the body becomes apparent. A simple pointing gesture to the same location that has been established for David makes repeating his name sign unnecessary. Localization is a common strategy in American Sign Language for establishing certain nouns for subsequent referencing. The name sign can also be used along with the pointed index finger.

complain The fingertips of the "CLAW" hands (bent "5" hands) are jabbed alternately against the chest. The accompanying facial expression will indicate discomfort. The chest-striking motion may be repeated several times to indicate that the complaining was a continuous or at least a repeated action in the past. The sign is similar to the sign for *uncomfortable*. In the latter, the fingertips of both "CLAW" hands are placed against the chest, and the body is wiggled and squirmed as the hands push against the body as if irritating it.

old The right "C" or "O" hand is placed under the chin and wiggled slightly as it is moved downward, tracing the outline of a beard. The motivation of the sign is lost here, as shoes are not likely to have beards. The left index finger may point downward to imaginary David's feet as the sign for *old* is executed. Such simultaneous execution of signs is not very common in American Sign Language, but it may be used for the sake of emphasis or as a literary or rhetorical device.

shoes hurt *Shoes* is signed as before. For hurt, the thumb nail of the right "A" hand may be pressed against the chin as the hand is rocked back and forth with twists of the wrist. The sign also means *suffer, patient, suffer patiently.* There is another sign for *pain* which could be used here: the index fingers of both hands are pointed toward each other and are then jabbed closer together with a twist of both wrists.

feet Again the right index finger is pointed downward twice, either to the signer's feet or, preferably, to imaginary David's feet.

Almost The left hand is held palm up in front of the body, and the right palm scrapes slowly up against the backs of the fingers of the left hand as the right palm is raised upward toward the face. The slow movement plus a pained facial expression help to convey the intended meaning.

all afternoon The sign for *all* may be used here: the left hand is held, palm up, in front of the body, and the right hand, beginning with the palm down, makes a sweeping circle, ending with the palm up as the back of the right hand is brought into the palm of the left. *Afternoon* is signed by holding the left arm horizontally across the front of the body, and the right forearm is rested against it as the right hand is brought down slowly in front of the body, imitating the descent of the sun in the afternoon sky. Instead of signing *all,* the notion of *all afternoon* may be conveyed simply by the slow and deliberate manner in which the sign for *afternoon* is executed.

use-up The left hand is held, palm down, in front of the body. The right hand is placed across the left wrist with the palm facing the body. As the right hand moves forward, scraping the little finger edge along the back of the left hand, the right hand closes into a fist. The movement is abrupt, and the final position shows the left hand in its initial position with the right hand as a clenched fist off to the right.

before The left hand is held with the palm facing forward in front of the body so as to establish a point of reference. An alternate form presents the left hand with the palm toward the body. The back of the right hand is placed near the left, palm toward the body, and the right hand is then brought toward the signer's body. This strategy effectively establishes a temporal frame of reference within the time frame in effect for the longer narrative. It was the better part of an afternoon that occurred two weeks ago that was used up *before* the signer succeeded in finding shoes. As an alternative, one could sign *All afternoon use-up, finally succeed. Finally* strikes the right index finger or the right little finger downward against the extended little finger of the left hand.

succeed The index fingers of both hands are pointed toward the head, and they are brought forward and upward with a twist of the wrist.

buy shoes can afford *Buy* and *shoes* are signed as indicated previously. *Can* is signed by bringing both fists, palms down, downward forcefully in front of the body. *Afford* is signed by tapping the tip of the right index finger in the middle of the left palm. The sign is related to *pay,* in which the right index finger is scraped outward along the left palm as if flipping money out.

First store The right index finger is struck against the upraised left thumb for *first. Store* is signed the same as *sell:* the "AND" hands are held in front of the body with the fingers pointing downward, and they are agitated by bending the wrists. It has been said that the sign is derived from the act of holding a garment up and shaking it out so that a shopper can inspect it. The same sign is also used for the verb, *sell.* The signs *First store* may be signed off to the left so as to make it clear that this store is not the one where the shoes were bought. *S-T-O-R-E* may be fingerspelled.

enter The left hand is held, palm down, in front of the body, and the right hand, palm down, is moved under it and out the other side.

nothing The right "0" hand is held under the chin, and the right hand is flung outward as it changes to a "5" hand. An alternative sign for *nothing* uses both "0" hands and flings them off to the side as they open to "5" hands.

below The left hand is held, palm down, in front of the body, and the right hand is placed with the back of the hand under the palm of the left. The right hand is then brought downward so as to be well *below* the left. The sign is similar in construction to the sign for *before* executed previously, only this time the two hands work together to indicate a spatial rather than a temporal relation.

$10 The numeral *ten* may be followed by the sign for *dollar*, in which the right thumb and fingers grasp the left hand, palm facing right, and scrape outward along the palm as if straightening out crumpled bills. Another version of the sign holds the left hand, palm up, and the thumb and fingers of the right hand grasp the fingertips repeatedly as they scrape off the edge of the hand. This sign resembles the act of peeling off bills as if taking them from the hand so as to give them to someone. If the sign for *ten* is executed with a sharp twist of the wrist, this is taken to mean *ten dollars*. The same strategy is used for other small sums of money. A hooked *five* means *$5*, and a hooked *three* means *$3*. Of course, odd sums or large sums of money will have to be indicated in some other way.

Second The right index finger is touched to the fingertip of the left "L" hand, palm up. There is an alternative manner of executing the ordinal numerals that might be used here: the numerals are presented with a slight twist of the wrist, not nearly as large a movement as is used for indicating sums of money. Thus, a twisted *one* is *first*, a twisted *two* is *second*, and a twisted *three* is *third*. This sequence of ordinal numerals can run all the way up to *ten (tenth)*. The other one, which forms the numeral on the left hand and touches the last finger of the numeral that is extended, can only be used up to *fourth* or *fifth*.

store have The sign for *store* is the same as before. *Have* is signed by touching the tips of the fingers of both hands to the chest. These signs may be executed midway between the area where *First store* and *Succeed buy shoes* were executed. Such localization of the three stores from left to right with the successful experience associated with the store on the right makes for a very smooth return to the main subject of the paragraph after the digression to the stores which proved to be unhelpful.

cheap shoes For *cheap* the left hand is held with the palm facing the right, and the right hand, palm up, is turned over so that it can scrape downward, palm down, along the palm of the left hand.

few The hands are held loosely as fists in front of the body, palms up, and the fingers are slowly unfurled, one at a time as the thumb rubs across each fingertip. The slowness of the execution of the sign indicates the small number of shoes present.

poor The left arm is held so that the left elbow can be grasped by the right hand. The right hand is pulled off the elbow one or more times. The sign is said to be derived from the holes in elbows that are likely to be found when people are poor. Like the English word, the sign *poor* may refer to poor quality as well as to limited financial resources.

no-good There are two common expressions in American Sign Language for *No-good*, both derived from fingerspelling. The one is derived from the one-hand alphabet, and the wrist rolls over as the right hand moves from the "N" to the "G" configuration. The other is derived from the two-hand alphabet. The index and middle fingers of the right hand are slapped into the left palm, and then the right fist is slapped into the same palm. Since the sign is used by deaf people who do not know or use the two-handed alphabet (it is common in Great Britain, but not in the United States or Canada), there is an alternate form that strikes the right index finger in the left palm followed by the fist.

Later The thumb of the right "L" hand is placed in the left palm, and the index finger of the right "L" hand is moved forward in an arc with the thumb pressed against the left hand serving as the axis. Again, using the left hand to provide a temporal frame of reference supercedes temporarily the time frame established for the entire narrative. The movement is forward, implying the future; but the future is relative to the previously futile search for shoes one afternoon two weeks ago.

succeed find shoes *Succeed* and *shoes* are signed as indicated previously. *Find* is signed by holding the left "C" hand, palm to the right, and the right hand, palm down, begins in an initial position below the left hand. As it rises it changes to a "F" hand just as it emerges through the opening of the left "C" hand. This sentence may now be signed off to the right again, indicating that we are now back in the store where the shoes were bought.

worth $6.50 The citation form of the sign for *worth* brings both "F" hands, palms facing, up in an arc so as to meet in front of the body, thumbs and index fingers touching. The basic meaning of the sign is *worth, value, worthy*. Here, for *worth, cost* the sign may be executed slightly differently. The two "F" hands may be touched together several times in front of the body as if to combine the signs for *worth* and *even* (*even* is signed by touching the fingertips of the bent "B" hands together several times in front of the body). For $6.50, the dollar amount is indicated as described previously: the numeral *six* is hooked in front of the right shoulder. Then the *fifty* is executed in the usual manner. Taken together, the sign is unambiguous, and it means *six dollars and fifty cents*.

Shoes true expensive The sign for *true* moves the upright right index finger from the lips forward from the face. The sign for expensive is a compound: *money + wow* (a general intensifier). *Money* is signed by tapping the back of the right "AND" hand in the left palm. *Wow* shakes the right "5" hand vigorously at the side of the body. When a compound is formed in American Sign Language, the first element generally loses some of its features. In this case, *money* is often executed with several taps of the right hand in the left. *Expensive* moves immediately from one tap of the right hand to the second element, *wow* (see Fig. 37).

To move out of the spatial frame of reference that has distinguished the three stores, this sentence is likely to make use of no localization at all. Instead, eye contact with the receiver will signal a new topic of conversation.

Me idea no For *me*, the right index finger is touched to the signer's chest. *Idea* is signed by hooking the right "I" hand upward from the right side of the forehead. The *no* following can be made more emphatic by executing it in the same location: the right "O" hand may be placed against the right side of the forehead and then brought straight out forcefully forward. The same sign for *no* may also originate from the side of the head so as to enlarge the area encompassed by its movement. An alternative sign for *no* places the two "O" hands together in front of the body and then moves them forcefully apart sideways. In the present text, signing it near the forehead so as to tie it to *idea* is a nice touch. An alternative sign for *no* strikes the right "O" hand against the left palm, which faces outward.

money　＋　wow　＝ expensive

FIG. **37.** *The sign* **wow** *or* **phew** *is an intensifier, adding emphasis to the sign that precedes it, as in* **money wow** *for* **expensive.**

Me expect *Me* is signed as before. *Expect* is a compound: *think* + a modification of *wait*. For *think* the right index finger is touched to the forehead. The sign for *wait* is ordinarily executed with both palms up as the fingers of both hands are bent or wiggled. In *expect, hope* the right hand is turned over, and the fingertips are waved toward each other. The hands are waved by bending them at the knuckles several times. Signed forcefully with an appropriate facial expression, the sign means *hope*.

look-around This is a modification of the sign for *look*, which is signed by placing the right "V" hand so that the fingers point to the eyes and then turning the "V" outward. This sign permits a number of variations, imitative of the kind of action that accompanies *looking*. One can *look up and down, look sideways, look back, look around,* etc. In this case after the "V" hand is turned outward, the hand could be dropped downward several times as it moves horizontally across the front of the signer as if looking up and down in the store windows of several shoe stores.

can find shoes good cheap The only sign in this phrase not used previously in this paragraph is the sign *good.* The fingertips of the right hand are touched to the lips, and the back of the right hand is then dropped down into the left palm.

Me wrong *Me* is signed as indicated previously. *Wrong* is signed by touching the fingers of the "Y" hand to the chin, palm toward the chin. For emphasis, the right "Y" hand may be twisted around on the chin from the right to the left side. The movement tends to emphasize the meaning: "I was really wrong."

Must The right "X" hand, palm down, is hooked sharply downward at the right side of the body. The force of the movement indicates the relative amount of emphasis. The same sign may also mean *should, ought.*

search The right "C" hand makes a small circular motion in front of the right eye. The head may be turned from side to side as if participating in the searching activity.

hard The right bent "V" hand is struck against the back of the left fist. The contact may be made between the knuckles of the "V" hand and the left fist, or the base of the right fist with the bent "V" hand extended upward may be struck against the back of the left fist.

Terrible The right "O," "F" or "8" hands are held next to the sides of the head, and they are thrown vigorously upward, changing to open "5" hands. In the present context the sign may be thrown forward in the direction that the person has been searching, or the signer may establish eye contact with the receiver and execute the sign at the sides of the head. The same sign also means *awful, horrible.*

Think The right index finger is jabbed to the forehead and held there. The force of the movement and holding the final position makes it a forceful imperative.

Clothes The fingertips of both "5" hands are brushed downward along the front of the chest one or more times.

Will The right hand, palm facing left and fingers pointing forward, is moved forward from the shoulder. This is the standard future marker for American Sign Language.

need new *Need* is the same sign as *must* used previously. *New* is signed as described earlier.

Think The sign for think is repeated, this time with a shocked facial expression. For variety, the sign may be executed with the left hand instead of the right. It would probably be signed more forcefully. An intensifier, such as *wow*, may be added for emphasis.

Me afraid think *Me* and *think* are signed as indicated previously. The emphasis in this phrase falls on the sign for afraid. Both "5" hands, palms toward the body, are held with the fingertips pointing toward each other. They are then moved forcefully toward each other so that the final position shows the wrists crossed and the "5" hands shielding the body. There is another sign for *fear, afraid* in which the hands are held with the palms outward as if warding off some sort of danger. They are waved back and forth as they retreat toward the body.

The body may also move backward as if retreating from the approaching danger.

Can foresee future *Can* is signed as indicated previously. *Foresee* is another variation on the theme of *see*. The left hand is held, palm down, over the eyes, and the right "V" hand is pointed first so that the fingertips point to the eyes, and then the hand is turned out and moved forward so that it passes under the left palm and out into the future. *Future* is the general future marker, the right hand, palm facing left, is moved forward from the right shoulder.

shirt The sign for shirt is similar to the sign for *clothes*. To distinguish *shirt* from *clothes* in general, the downward movement may be shorter, or the person may brush higher up on the shoulder. Incidentally, it is not unusual for deaf persons to speak the words as they sign them, even though their speech may not always be clearly intelligible. In this case, the lip movements associated with the word *shirt* are quite plain, and the speech may assist in making the message understood. Just because deaf persons use American Sign Language does not mean that they make no use of speech. Very often they use both together, speaking and signing at the same time.

$8 The numeral, *8*, is hooked downward and to the left. The sign for *dollar* may be added.

Coat The thumbs of both "A" hands trace the lapels of an imaginary coat on both sides of the chest.

forty five dollar *Forty five* is signed by forming the numerals *four* and *five* on the right hand. The hand may move to the left for the *4* and to the right for the *5*. *Dollar* is signed as indicated previously. The 45 automatically pluralizes the noun, *dollar*.

Happen Both hands are held with the index fingers extended. They are turned over so that the palms face down and the index fingers point forward, parallel to one another. Since this is a question, it will be marked by raised eyebrows and by holding the terminal position of the sign for a longer time than is usual.

Know you For *know* the fingertips of the right hand are tapped to the forehead. *You*

points the index finger toward the receiver. For special effect, the two signs can be executed simultaneously. That is, the left index finger can be pointing to the receiver all the time that the right hand is tapping the forehead.

(D) will get new clothes All of these signs have been used previously in this narrative except *get*. *Get* is signed by holding both "5" hand out in front of the body, and they are brought together toward the body, ending as "S" hands the right on top of the left.

Me same Same is signed either by placing the right "Y" hand, palm down, first in one location and then in another, or by aligning both index fingers alongside each other, palms down. The index fingers may be bumped against each other two or more times.

last year This is a special modulation of the sign for *year*. Ordinarily, *year* is signed by forming two "S" hands, and the right "S" hand, probably representing the earth revolving around the sun, makes a complete circle over and under the left fist, ending with the right "S" hand resting on top of the left. For *last year,* the circle around the left fist is omitted. Instead, the right "S" hand is bumped against the top of the left "S" hand, and then the right hand is moved back over the right shoulder as the numeral *one* is formed on the hand. By a similar modulation, one can indicate *two years ago,* and *three years ago*. If, instead of moving back over the right shoulder, the numeral *one* is moved forward from the body, the meaning is *one year from now,* or *next year*. With the numerals *two* and *three* the meaning is *two years from now* and *three years from now*.

Maybe The two hands are held, palms up, in front of the body, and they are moved up and down alternately in an indecisive manner. In this case, the indecision is nullified by a facial expression that indicates interest in considering the possibility that is about to be expressed.

me gain For *me* the index finger is pointed to the chest. *Gain* may be signed by using the sign for *add:* the left hand is held, palm down, with the index and middle fingers extended, and the right hand, with the same hand configuration, begins palm up in front of the body, and is raised up and over the left hand, and then is brought down so that the finger tips of the right hand come into contact with the backs of the index and middle fingers of the left hand. The effect is one of having the index and middle fingers of the right hand pile something on top of the backs of the index and middle fingers of the left hand.

ten pounds For *ten* the upraised thumb of the right "A" hand is wiggled slightly. Pounds is signed the same as *weigh:* The left hand is held with the index finger extended, palm to the right, and the right index finger is placed across the left index finger and rocked as if teetering on the left finger. The sign probably represents the arm of a balance scale rocking back and forth when something is being weighed.

Then The left "L" hand is held with the palm to the right, thumb up, and the right index finger is touched first to the thumb and then to the top edge of the extended left index finger.

can say Can is signed as indicated previously. For *say* the right index finger is moved in a small circular motion forward from the mouth several times. The same sign also means *speak, talk,* and, with a very special significance for deaf people, *a hearing person.* If a deaf person asks, *You speak?* What he means is, "Are you a hearing person?" It may or may not be a compliment, depending on the situation. One who is not a member of a minority group cannot expect to be accepted as an equal regardless of the circumstances. Hearing people need to realize that deaf people appreciate their good will, and even are generally grateful for any assistance that they might render. But deaf people have to put up with a great deal of well-intentioned nonsense. Hearing people who want to "help the deaf" may discover to their dismay that intrusions in the affairs of the deaf community may not always be appreciated. Especially inappropriate is any attempt on the part of hearing persons to "help" the deaf by doing things for them that they can do quite well for themselves. Paternalism is not helpful.

me grow "" *Grow* is signed by holding the left "O" hand in front of the body with the opening up, and the right "AND" hand, fingers first, is thrust up through the opening as the right hand changes into the "5" configuration. The sign resembles something coming up from the ground and then spreading its leaves. After the sign for *grow* the signer may make quotation marks in the air with the bent "V" hands, wiggling the fingers often enough to make it plain that these are marks in the air signifying quotation marks. This gesture has the same implication as the English expression; indeed, it may be derived from the English usage. It implies that the signer is knowingly using the sign "grow" as a figure of speech. The signer may wink or indicate by some other means that he is being facetious.

Also This sign is the same as the one previously recommended for *same:* the right "Y" hand, palm down, is moved downward in two different locations. In this case, since David has been localized to the left of the signer, it is appropriate that the hand be placed down first in David's location and then directly in front of the signer. This serves to indicate that David and the signer are judged to be *similar* in some respect. The other sign for *same,* the horizontal index fingers placed parallel to one another in front of the body, may also be used.

need new clothes All three of these signs have been described previously. The signer may nod his head in obvious agreement with what he is now suggesting. Such body movements and facial expressions contribute considerably to the meaning of statements in American Sign Language. In this case, the nodding head serves to indicate how the signer feels about the message that he is transmitting, namely, that he is in complete agreement with it.

98

VOCABULARY ————————————————

1. add (HH-38)
2. afford (see text)
3. afraid (HH-48, TO-177)
4. afternoon (HH-402, TO-185)
5. ago (HH-118, TO-205)
6. all (HH-494, TO-193)
7. almost (HH-428, TO-56)
8. also (HH-452, TO-104)
9. awful (HH-296, TO-548)
10. baby (HH-478, TO-273)
11. before (HH-30, TO-204)
12. below (HH-15, TO-36)
13. big (HH-473, TO-429)
14. bring (HH-91, TO-52)
15. brother (HH-238, TO-107)
16. buy (HH-447, TO-66)
17. can (HH-72, TO-155)
18. carry (HH-91, TO-52)
19. center (HH-449, TO-384)
20. cheap (TO-68)
21. city (HH-154, TO-351)
22. clothes (HH-313, TO-172)
23. coat (HH-313, TO-172)
24. complain (HH-300, TO-150)
25. cost (see text)
26. David (see text)
27. dollar (HH-319, TO-65)
28. downtown (HH-449, TO-384)
29. during (HH-174, TO-102)
30. eight dollars (see text)
31. enter (HH-242, TO-37)
32. even (HH-73, TO-363)
33. expect (HH-12, TO-454)
34. expensive (HH-447, TO-69)
35. feet (see text)
36. few (HH-496, TO-240)
37. fifty (TO-p.5)
38. finally (HH-288, TO-423)
39. find (HH-258, TO-501)
40. first (HH-116, TO-515)
41. five dollars (see text)
42. for (HH-404, TO-18)
43. foresee (see text)
44. forty-five (TO-p.5)
45. future (HH-360, TO-201)

46. gain (HH-38)
47. get (HH-445, TO-604)
48. good (HH-342, TO-259)
49. grow (HH-364, TO-487)
50. happen (HH-174, TO-228)
51. hard (HH-367, TO-302)
52. have (HH-292, TO-268)
53. he (HH-403)
54. hearing person (HH-383, TO-216)
55. her (HH-469)
56. hers (HH-469)
57. his (HH-469)
58. hope (HH-12, TO-454)
59. horrible (HH-296, TO-548)
60. hurt (HH-13, TO-101)
61. husband (HH-238 + 248, TO-409)
62. idea (HH-134, TO-418)
63. in (HH-242, TO-14)
64. inch (see text)
65. know (HH-14, TO-206)
66. large (HH-473, TO-429)
67. last week (HH-10, TO-464)
68. last year (HH-349)
69. later (HH-262, TO-531)
70. look around (HH-413)
71. look back (HH-413)
72. look sideways (HH-413)
73. look up and down (HH-413)
74. male (HH-238, TO-105)
75. marry (HH-248, TO-405)
76. maybe (HH-19, TO-51)
77. me (HH-192, TO-2)
78. middle (HH-449, TO-384)
79. money (HH-447, TO-63)
80. month (HH-482, TO-317)
81. much (HH-473, TO-167)
82. must (HH-62, TO-628)
83. my (HH-307, TO-6)
84. need (HH-62, TO-628)
85. new (HH-212, TO-74)
86. next year (HH-497, TO-296)
87. none (HH-392, TO-40)
88. no good (fingerspell)
89. nothing (HH-392, TO-40)
90. old (HH-110, TO-485)

91. ought (HH-62, TO-628)
92. pain (HH-344, TO-320)
93. past (HH-118, TO-205)
94. patient (HH-13, TO-101)
95. pay (HH-126, TO-467)
96. poor (HH-324, TO-329)
97. pound (HH-215, TO-618)
98. prophesy (see text)
99. rock (HH-232)
100. same (HH-452, TO-104)
101. say (HH-383, TO-216)
102. search (HH-41, TO-401)
103. second (HH-116)
104. seem (HH-363, TO-203)
105. shirt (see text)
106. shoes (HH-253, TO-152)
107. shop (TO-66)
108. should (HH-62, TO-628)
109. similar (HH-452, TO-104)
110. since (HH-346, TO-103)
111. six (TO-p.4)
112. son (HH-478, TO-274)
113. speak (HH-383, TO-216)
114. store (HH-78, TO-242)
115. succeed (HH-486, TO-230)
116. suffer (HH-13, TO-101)
117. take (see text)
118. talk (HH-383, TO-216)

119. ten (TO-p.4)
120. ten dollars (see text)
121. tenth (see text)
122. terrible (HH-296, TO-548)
123. their (HH-469)
124. then (TO-461)
125. think (HH-226, TO-79)
126. third (see text)
127. three dollars (see text)
128. three years ago (HH-349)
129. true (HH-291, TO-219)
130. two years ago (HH-349)
131. uncomfortable (HH-300)
132. use up (HH-393, TO-490)
133. value (HH-343, TO-542)
134. very (HH-473, TO-313)
135. wait (HH-435, TO-169)
136. week (HH-326, TO-462)
137. weigh (HH-215, TO-618)
138. what for? (HH-404, TO-18)
139. while (HH-174, TO-102)
140. will (HH-360, TO-201)
141. worth (HH-343, TO-542)
142. wow (HH-81)
143. wrong (HH-243, TO-644)
144. you (HH-403, TO-3)
145. your (HH-469, TO-8)

EXERCISES

Sign the following sentences and provide an English translation.

1. Downtown in city have store big, store have clothes much.
2. David complain, complain son marry; David he must pay, expensive.
3. My brother know man, brother carry baby man his.
4. You should know clothes value clothes you need shop shop get cheap.
5. Three years ago me buy shirt cost $5. Last week same shirt cost $10.
6. $8 $10 same; can afford nothing.
7. My clothes all poor; need new.
8. My brother say next year he will succeed, will have money much.
9. My son complain money use up; need $10; what for? He say clothes. You think?
10. Good idea look around buy clothes, search clothes good.

Lesson Nine

ENGLISH ORIGINAL

My Job Application

I applied for a job Monday, and I was surprised at how many questions they asked me. I had to fill out a long form with all kinds of questions on it about my family, my schooling, and my previous work experience. They wanted to know whether I lived with my parents, how many brothers and sisters I had, when I finished school, and all kinds of things. Wow! When I was finished, I felt that I had written the story of my life. I certainly had no secrets any more. I don't understand why they have to make people write so much before they will hire them. I think it is a waste of time.

SIGN LANGUAGE GLOSS

My Apply Work

Monday apply work. Me surprise many many question, question, question they question me. Must write on paper long; must explain about my family, my school, my work before. Want know, (question) where you live? With father mother? (pause) Brother sister how—many? (pause) When finish school? (pause) Work before, what-do? Various—things. Phew! Write, write, write (pause) finish (pause) my include life there. Secret me none. Why force people write, write, write before hire? What-for? What-for? Think me waste time.

GRAMMATICAL NOTES

Monday The days of the week are initialized signs (see Fig. 38). For *Monday* the right "M" hand makes a small circle in front of the right shoulder. The palm may face inward for casual usage or outward for more formal usage. *Tuesday, Wednesday, Friday* and *Saturday* are signed similarly. *Thursday* is a minor exception: after the "T" is formed on the right hand, it is the right "H" hand that is circled so as to distinguish it from *Tuesday. Sunday* is signed altogether differently: The open palms are circled in opposite directions as they face outward in front of the face.

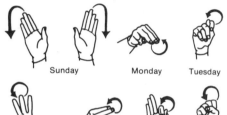

Sunday   Monday   Tuesday

Wednesday   Thursday   Friday   Saturday

FIG. **38.** *The days of the week, except for Sunday, are initialized signs.*

Since this was a past event, the sign for *Monday* may be executed over the right shoulder rather than in front of the shoulder so as to add a past marker to the sign. This would fix the meaning more specifically as *This past Monday.*

apply Since the past tense has already been established by the time marker associated with the sign, *Monday,* a time marker is not needed for the verb, *apply.* The sign commonly used for *apply* in the sense of a formal job application is the same sign as is used for *signature* or *sign your name:* the fingertips of the right "H" hand are slapped onto the edge of the upturned left palm. If the job application involved filling out a form, the sign may be repeated several times as the left hand is moved slightly downward as if following a printed page. There is another sign that might be used

for *apply* in the sense of *volunteer:* The right thumb and index finger tug at the right lapel of a coat or shirt as if to pull the applicant forward. The subject, *I,* is understood.

work Unless J-O-B is fingerspelled, the same sign would be used for the noun as for the verb, *work.* The right fist, palm down, is knocked against the back of the left fist. Of course, in English, too, the same word, *work,* can be either a noun or a verb, depending on how it is used in a sentence. Criteria for deciding the part of speech that should be assigned to specific English words are relatively easy to master and to use with some confidence. The form classes of signs and their role in American Sign Language sentences are areas of interest for current linguistic study.

Me The same sign may be used for the first person personal pronoun whether it is the subject or the object of a sentence. The index finger is simply pointed to the chest of the signer. There is an initialized sign for *I* derived from the English pronoun: The thumb of the right "I" hand is tapped to the signer's chest.

surprise This sign is motivated by the facial expression of a surprised person; he is likely to open his eyes quickly. The thumb and index finger of both hands are touched together and held next to the eyes at both sides of the head. They are then spread apart quickly as the eyes are opened widely. The same sign executed more slowly means *awaken.* A past tense marker is not inserted after *surprise* because the past tense has already been indicated previously.

many many The sign for *many* flicks the fingers of one or both fists outward one or more times. The sign is often repeated several times. If the fingers of one or both hands are unfurled slowly instead of being flicked out quickly, the sign means *few.*

question The sign for *question* traces a question mark in the air with one or both index fingers. To represent an ongoing activity or a plurality of questions, the sign may be repeated several times. A variant of the sign ends with spread "5" hands and means *test, examination.* As depicted in Fig. 39, the sign is executed toward the location established for the object.

FIG. **39.** *The sign for question is directed to the verb's object.*

they There is no specific sign for the third person plural pronoun. A natural gesture with the right hand, palm up thrown forward in the general direction of the imaginary inquisitors is sufficient.

question me Some signs can be made reflexive by directing them toward the signer's body, as illustrated in Fig. 40. This is an example of such a sign. Previously the question marks were traced in the air outward from the signer. Now they are turned toward the signer, suggesting that the questions are being directed to him. The sign *me* is gratuitous, but it may be added.

FIG. **40.** *Some signs may have their movements altered in such a way that when they are directed toward the signer they imply a reflexive.*

Must *Must* is a conventional sign for *compulsion.* The right "X" hand, palm down, is brought sharply downward in front of the body. The force of the movement indicates the degree of compulsion present, and the accompanying facial expression, body posture, and other cues indicate how the signer feels about being coerced.

write This is an imitative sign: The right hand holds an imaginary pencil, and the signer acts out writing in the left palm.

on Prepositions dealing with spatial relations are generally indicated in American Sign Language by allowing the left hand to provide a point of reference. The meaning is then conveyed by the location or movement of the right hand in relation to the left. In this case, the fingertips of the right hand are tapped on the top of the back of the left fist. In an alternate version, the right palm is rested on the back of the left fist.

paper It has been suggested that this sign is derived from the way in which paper emerges from a printing press. The left hand is held, palm up, in front of the body, and the heel of the right palm is struck against the heel of the left palm several times as the right hand moves toward the left across the body. This is a plausible explanation, especially since many deaf people have worked in the printing trades. However, explanations advanced to account for the origin or motivation of signs may be fanciful post hoc accounts rather than genuine history. They should be taken with a grain of salt. Many instructors provide such information because it may help a student remember the sign.

long There is a sign for *long* in the sense of *long time* which draws the index fingertip of the right "L" hand up the length of the left forearm. Since filling out a complicated form undoubtedly requires a long time, that sign could be used here. As an alternative, the left hand can be held, palm up, in front of the face, and the right "L" hand may sweep down the left palm and arm toward the body. Or, the two "L" hands may be drawn apart from each other in front of the body as if stretching from the floor to the ceiling (see Fig. 41). In American Sign Language the adjective often follows the noun that it modifies. This may reflect some influence from the French language, since the Abbe de l'Epee followed French word order in developing the "Methodical Sign Language" which became the model for the first Sign Language used for educational purposes in the United States. It is also possible that a visual language finds it more natural first to identify the noun that is to be described and then to add the descriptive adjective or adjectives.

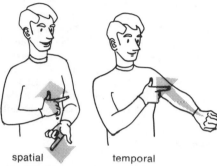

spatial   temporal

FIG. 41. Long *may be signed in a variety of ways, depending to some extent on whether the meaning is temporal or spatial.*

explain This is one of several related signs executed with the same hand configurations and in the same location but with slightly different movements. The basic hand configuration has the thumb and index finger of both hands touching or brought together repeatedly so as to touch one another. The other fingers are extended, so that the hand configuration could be described as "F" hands. For *explain, tell a story, explanation* both hands are brought together in front of the body, and just as the thumbs and fingers come into contact with each other and with the thumb and finger of the other hand, they are drawn apart again. The movement is repeated several times. If the hands continue moving apart from one another in a waving motion after the initial contact, the sign means *sentence.* If the "F" hands are held so that the tips of the thumbs and index fingers of opposite hands are almost touching and then rocked alternately back

and forth around that central focus, the sign means *interpret.* Among specialists in the area of deafness, this term has the special meaning of *interpreting* from English into Sign Language. Professional interpreters for the deaf make a distinction between *interpreting,* which requires some latitude for paraphrasing and providing necessary background information, and *translating,* which is presumed to remain more faithful to the English original. To distinguish between interpreting from English to Signs and from Signs to English, the latter is sometimes called "reverse interpreting." Since reverse interpreting requires considerable fluency in American Sign Language, interpreters who are able to serve in this capacity are in relatively short supply. There is a national organization, the Registry of Interpreters for the Deaf (R.I.D.) with headquarters at 814 Thayer Ave., Silver Spring, MD 20910, devoted to improving the quality of interpreting services available to deaf people. In addition, a consortium of institutions, strategically located across the country, has instituted specialized training programs for interpreters. Information on the consortium can be obtained by writing to Consortium on Interpreter Training, Gallaudet College, Washington, D.C., 20002.

about This preposition follows the same principle as *on.* The right index finger traces a small circle around the fingertips of the left "AND" hand.

my The open palm is the possessive marker in American Sign Language. Placed against the signer's chest it means *my.*

family There is an initialized sign for *family:* the sign for *group* is executed with cupped "C" hands moved so as to enclose an imaginary group. Signed with "F" hands, the meaning is *family.* Deaf persons who have incorporated this initialized sign into their manual language vocabulary are likely to use it. Those who have not may sign *home,* instead. Initialized signs are complex symbols designed to reference fields of meaning in two language systems at the same time. They derive two of their distinctive features, their location and their movement, from traditional American Sign

Language usage, and they modify their third distinctive feature, the hand configuration, so that the sign can simultaneously refer to a related English word. Most initialized signs incorporate the first letter of the intended English word, although some recently developed innovations make use of a different letter, for example, *truly* signed with the "R" hand for *are*. Initialized signs are widely used in American Sign Language, and a cursory check through any American Sign Language dictionary will turn up a large number of signs whose hand configuration is a letter of the one-hand manual alphabet that seems to have been influenced by the spelling of a related English word. Moreover, there have been recurring reform movements designed to modify colloquial Sign Languages so as to make them more compatible with the language spoken by the larger society, and these have often made use of initialization in an attempt at developing a one-to-one correspondence between signs and words. The prevalence of initializing in American Sign Language offers a special challenge to linguistic study, since there is no comparable linguistic usage in spoken languages in which the lexicon of one language is modified so that it can reference, in part, the lexicon of another while retaining enough of its original form, especially its movement and location, so that it might remain intelligible to native speakers.

school This sign has been said to be derived from the custom of teachers to clap their hands in order to gain their pupils' attention.

work before *Before* makes use of the time line running horizontally in front of the body. Movements toward the body represent times past, while movements forward across the time line represent times in the future. In this case, the time line is supplemented by the left hand, which provides a point of reference for the right. Ordinarily, such a point of reference is used primarily with signs referring to spatial relations, especially prepositions. The same strategy is sometimes used for temporal relations. Thus, the sign *before*, referring to time, can also mean *on this side*,

referring to a spatial location, and the sign *after*, referring to time, can also mean *across, go across*, referring to space. In *work before* the sign obviously has temporal significance. If the right hand is drawn back from the left in an exaggerated motion extending over the right shoulder, the sign means *all previous work experience*. If the signer does not wish to emphasize the need for completeness in the account, the movement can be restricted to the space between the left hand and the signer's body.

Want know While these two signs can be executed successively, American Sign Language allows for some simultaneity, and this is an instance where simultaneously executed gestures are permissible. The sign for *want* can be executed with the left hand at the same time as the sign for *know* is executed with the right hand.

question One of the powerful and effective strategies that American Sign Language has available is role playing. Often the signer will take the role of other characters in a narrative, letting his facial expression and body posture convey information about the way in which the various people feel about what is being said or done, while the signs he executes serve as "lines" in the play he is dramatizing. In the present context, it is even permissible for the signer to pretend that he is the person who, through the form, is asking the questions of the job applicant. Or, it might be argued that the signer is personifying the application form and allowing it to interrogate the applicant (himself). Role taking with direct discourse replaces the indirect discourse of other languages, for which American Sign Language has no counterpart. Taking the role of the speaker is the most direct approach available, even when it requires that the identity of the signer be preserved in the form of an imaginary character also occupying the stage on which the action is set.

where A common sign for *where* simply waggles the upraised right index finger at the receiver. The same sign also means *Huh? What?* Since the signer has chosen, in this case, to personify the application form, he will address this question to his imaginary self, seated in front of the examiner, whose role he is taking.

you This sign is also addressed to the imaginary job applicant seated in front of the examiner.

live The sign for *live* is made by drawing both fists up the sides of the body. The sign may be initialized with "L" hands. The same sign may also mean *address*. No special marker is needed to indicate that this is a question. The facial expression and the expectant body posture after the question is asked, as if awaiting an answer, are sufficient. In any case, the context suggests that a number of questions will follow.

with Both fists are placed side by side for this sign. If they are moved forward from the body, the sign becomes a verb, *accompany, go with.*

father mother There is no special sign for *parent* or *parents* in American Sign Language. An initialized sign has been proposed which uses the male and female gender markers: the right "P" hand is touched to the forehead and the chin or moved down the right side of the head from the temple to the jaw. But the initialized sign is not in widespread use; when, the signs for *father* and *mother* are signed in quick succession, *parents* is understood. A pause here marks the end of the question and sets the stage for the next one.

brother   sister

FIG. **42.** *The compounds formed by adding* **same** *to the male and female gender signs mean* **brother** *and* **sister.**

brother sister These signs are compounds: *male + same = brother, female + same = sister.* The sign for *same* may be executed with the index fingers placed side by side, or the right hand with the index finger extended may be touched to the top of the left hand, index finger extended (see Fig. 42).

how many? If the sign for *many* is executed with a questioning expression, such as an arched eyebrow or open mouth, and held in the final position as if expecting an answer, the sign means *how many?* Dramatic changes in meaning such as this which are brought about by the accompanying facial expression or body posture illustrate the point that American Sign Language is not just a "hand language." American Sign Language involves the entire body both as an instrument for constructing gesture symbols by means of the hands and arms and also as a symbol itself, which conveys additional meaning by displaying or enacting it. Subtle cues associated with muscle tone, body stance, angle of body orientation, line of vision, etc., may be much more central aspects of manual language systems than they are of spoken languages. By means of such devices, deaf persons adapt a basic set of gesture symbols to a wide variety of situations and contexts, and they seem to be able to convey as subtle a range of nuances and shades of meaning as hearing persons do with spoken languages.

when This preposition is signed by extending the left index finger forward and then tracing a circle around it with the index finger of the right hand. The right fingertip is touched to the left fingertip in the final position.

finish school If the question were to be made completely unambiguous, it might be signed, *finish school* (pause) *finish when.* This sequence could be translated, "You have finished school, have you not? If so, when?" Another reason for signing *finish school* before signing *when* is that American Sign Language often has a preference for indicating the subject matter before elaborating on it. If it is first made clear that it is the applicant's completion of his schooling that is at issue, the question, *when*, would be quite clear.

work before These signs are executed as described previously.

what-do While clearly influenced by English, this colloquial expression has become well established in American Sign Language usage. The thumb of one or both hands is touched to the middle fingertip, and the index finger is brought into contact with the thumb repeatedly in an abbreviated spelling of DO, DO, DO, DO. In this context, the sign would be repeated several times, the signer would look directly at the imagined receiver, and the facial expression would be an expectant one, as if awaiting a reply. The same sign in other contexts might imply overwhelming boredom, much as the young child might pester his parents by asking repeatedly, *What can I do?*.

Various things The index fingers of both hands are tapped downward as the hands move apart from one another in front of the body, as if they are touching and, therefore, enumerating the "various things" that the signer has in mind.

Phew This sign is executed by shaking the right "5" hand off to the side of the body. It is a general intensifier. *Hot + phew = very hot. Money + phew = expensive. Work + phew = hard work.* In this discourse, the sign, *phew*, helps to break off the role playing, which has been in effect for some time. Clearly, this expression describes how the person feels who is on the receiving end of all of the questions.

Write, write, write Here the signer is enacting the activity associated with filling out the form. The repetition together with the pause imply that the job is being carried out to its completion.

finish The signer may straighten up at this point to show by his body posture that he is happy to have the job done.

my The open palm marks the possessive in American Sign Language. Placed against the chest, it means *my*. Directed outward it can mean *your, yours, his, her, hers, their,* or *theirs.*

include The left hand is held in a neutral position in front of the body, and the right hand, palm down, makes a sweeping gesture first off to the right and then back toward the left hand. As it reaches the left hand, the left hand grasps the fingers of the right hand firmly and holds on to them.

life The sign for the noun, *life,* is the same as for the verb, *live.* The "L" hands or "A" hands are brought up the chest.

there This is a natural gesture in which the right hand is dropped downward toward the front of the signer where the papers are imagined to be that he has been filling out.

Secret me none The sequence here follows the general rule that the subject matter of the discourse is indicated first, and then additional descriptive information is supplied. *Secret* is signed by pressing the thumbnail of the right "A" hand to the lips. *None* brings the "O" hands apart in front of the chest.

Why force write write write before hire? The interrogative *Why* could go at the end: *Force write write write why?* In this case, however, the signer has saved a stronger expression for the end: *What for? Why* is signed by holding the right hand with the palm facing the forehead. The right hand is moved forward from the face and changed to a "Y" hand. *Force* shoves the right "C" hand over the wrist of the horizontal left forearm.

before hire The sign for *hire* is related to the sign for *introduce.* For *hire* the right hand, palm up, is brought toward the body. For *introduce* both hands, palms up, are brought together in front of the body as if bringing two people together.

What-for? What-for? The sign here is the same as *for,* implying purpose. Signed with a questioning expression and repeatedly, it becomes a question, *What for? For what purpose?* The signer's gaze may dart around as he repeats the sign as if looking in vain for someone who will tell him. It is a rhetorical

question in this context. There is a colloquial expression in American Sign Language similar to the English, "Why must
they stick their nose in my business?" The
right index finger is touched to the nose
and then stuck into the left "O" hand; *Nose
stick-in paper my life, why.*

Think me While the reverse word order
compared to English is probably preferred
here, the opposite order is permissible, *Me
think. Think* touches the right index finger
to the forehead.

Waste time The sign for *waste* is probably
derived from the sign for *money.* The back
of the right hand is tapped into the left
palm for *money,* sometimes with the fingers
of the right hand clustered together as in
the "AND" hand configuration. In *waste*
the right hand is thrown out from the left
palm as it changes to the "5" position, as if
scattering everything in the palm to the
four winds. *Time* would probably be signed
by simply touching the right index finger
to the top of the left wrist, where a watch is
likely to be worn. There is another sign for
time in a general sense, in which the right
"T" hand is made to execute a circle on the
face of the left palm, facing forward.
Purists might argue that the second sign is
the "correct" one in this context, but either
sign is likely to be used, depending on the
signer's preference.

VOCABULARY

1. about (HH-39, TO-110)
2. accompany (HH-476, TO-19)
3. across (HH-209, TO-46)
4. address (HH-446, TO-119)
5. after (HH-209, TO-270)
6. all (HH-494, TO-193)
7. apply (HH-427, TO-500)
8. awaken (HH-207, TO-664)
9. before (HH-30, TO-204)
10. brother (HH-238, TO-107)
11. compulsion (HH-62, TO-628)
12. examination (HH-436)
13. expensive (HH-447, TO-69)
14. explain (HH-216, TO-545)
15. explanation (HH-216, TO-545)
16. family (HH-421)
17. father (HH-160, TO-140)
18. female (HH-500, TO-106)
19. few (HH-496, TO-240)
20. finish (HH-214, TO-174)
21. force (HH-355)
22. Friday (HH-328, TO-267)
23. go across (HH-209, TO-46)
24. go with (HH-476, TO-19)
25. group (HH-421, TO-412)
26. her (HH-410)
27. hers (HH-410)
28. hire (TO-355)
29. his (HH-410)
30. hot (HH-498, TO-136)
31. how many? (HH-34, TO-658)
32. huh? (HH-183, TO-28)
33. I (HH-70, TO-1)
34. include (HH-242, TO-194)
35. interpret (HH-90)
36. interpreting (HH-90)
37. introduce (HH-261, TO-354)
38. job (fingerspell)
39. know (HH-14, TO-206)
40. life (HH-446, TO-120)
41. live (HH-446, TO-119)
42. long (HH-297, TO-81)
43. long time (HH-297, TO-81)
44. male (HH-238, TO-105)
45. many (HH-34, TO-657)
46. me (HH-192, TO-2)
47. Monday (HH-328, TO-267)
48. money (HH-447, TO-63)
49. mother (HH-488, TO-138)
50. must (HH-62, TO-628)
51. my (HH-307, TO-6)
52. none (HH-392, TO-41)
53. nose (see text)
54. OK (fingerspell)
55. on (HH-200, TO-17)
56. on this side (HH-30, TO-369)
57. paper (HH-464, TO-59)
58. parents (TO-142)
59. people (HH-320, TO-427)
60. phew (HH-81)
61. question (HH-436, TO-631)
62. same (HH-452, TO-104)
63. Saturday (HH-328, TO-267)
64. school (HH-277, TO-49)
65. secret (HH-420, TO-100)
67. sign your name (HH-427, TO-500)
68. signature (HH-427, TO-500)
69. sister (HH-500, TO-108)
70. stick in (see text)
71. Sunday (HH-322, TO-266)
72. surprise (HH-207, TO-664)
73. tell a story (HH-216, TO-553)
74. test (HH-436, TO-630)
75. their (HH-469)
76. theirs (HH-469)
77. there (TO-727)
78. they (HH-403)
79. think (HH-226, TO-79)
80. Thursday (HH-328, TO-267)
81. time (HH-187, TO-595)
82. translating (HH-90)
83. truly (HH-291, TO-219)
84. Tuesday (HH-328, TO-267)
85. various things (HH-96, TO-322)
86. volunteer (HH-131, TO-555)
87. want (HH-448, TO-173)
88. waste (HH-7, TO-70)
89. Wednesday (HH-328, TO-267)
90. what? (HH-183, TO-28)

91. what do? (fingerspell D-O, D-O, D-O)
92. what for? (HH-404, TO-18)
93. when? (HH-180, TO-32)
94. where (HH-183, TO-28)
95. why? (HH-8, TO-16)
96. with (HH-476, TO-20)
97. work (HH-86, TO-161)
98. write (HH-359, TO-583)
99. you (HH-403, TO-3)
100. your (HH-460, TO-8)
101. yours (HH-460, TO-8)

EXERCISES

Sign the following sentences and provide an English translation.

1. Brother my need money, want car.
2. You nose stick-in my life, finish.
3. My mother interpret for me many time past; now not need.
4. Me must sign paper. Father go-with. First father see. OK? Me sign.
5. Mother go hospital. Why? Brother know. Will explain tomorrow.
6. All-day Friday must work, work, work; Saturday will loaf.
7. Mother ask me: Last Sunday, what-do? Why must all time explain, explain? What-for? My life; my secret.
8. Every day father come home from work, arrive same time.
9. You want work hospital? Must work hard. Accept? OK, go apply.
10. Ago Monday hot, phew!

Lesson Ten

ENGLISH TRANSLATION

My Visit to Ohio

Last Wednesday I flew to Ohio from Washington, D.C. A man named Harry, a friend of mine, invited me to make a television film. I liked the idea, so I agreed. It was a long flight, three hours, rather tiring. I read a book, but I was bored. Anyway, when I arrived here in Ohio, Harry met me in his truck and we drove to his home. He has a nice place, rather large. After we arrived we sat and talked, had a drink, and talked some more. It was enjoyable, but by that time it was one o'clock at night. I was afraid that I might oversleep the next morning. I always get up at 7:00. The next morning after a shower and a shave we drove to the television studio. It is really nice. They have a lot of equipment that I had never seen before. They had several cameras, at least four. During the television filming I tried to fingerspell some big words, and I discovered that I am a lousy speller. After the movie was over, I wanted to see some of the university campus. I visited and looked around. I hope some day that I will fly to Ohio again.

SIGN LANGUAGE ORIGINAL[1]

LITERAL GLOSS

My Visit to Ohio

Ago Wednesday me fly to O-H-I-O from Washington, D.C. What-for? What-for? Me man have friend man name H-A-R-R-Y. He invite me for make T-V T-V movie. Me like, O-K, accept. All right. Me fly long, three hour, fly fly fly fly. Me tired. Sit, read book. Read. Me bored. Anyway, me arrive here O-H-I-O. He H-A-R-R-Y he have truck, big truck. We-two drive his home. Truly nice, big. We-two arrive, sit, talk, drink, converse. Enjoy. True night, time one, night. Me afraid morning oversleep. Me afraid. Me get-up time seven. (Pause) Me bathe, finish, shave, finish. We-two drive for T-V T-V place building. True nice. But me machinery much me not-yet see before. Me surprise. Have one, two, three, four list for C-A-M-E-R-A. Have many many. T-V T-V movie me try fingerspell big-word. Me dummy fingerspell me. Movie finish, me want see school around area. Me visit, look. Me hope later will fly again O-H-I-O.

---

[1]Unlike the other lessons in this text, this lesson was prepared by beginning with an American Sign Language original, prepared by Dennis Cokely, who also served as a model for the videotapes tied to this manual. This is a literal gloss of Cokely's remarks. The English translation appearing with it was done last. Bernard Bragg (personal communication) has suggested that procedures like these ought to be as useful for teaching English to deaf persons as they are for teaching American Sign Language to hearing persons.

Ago Wednesday The temporal frame of reference is established at the outset as this past Wednesday. To show that it is the immediately previous Wednesday and not just any Wednesday in the past, the face is squinted as the sign *ago* is executed. *Ago* is the general past marker; the right hand is moved back over the right shoulder. *Wednesday* is signed by circling the letter "W" at shoulder height.

me fly *Me* is the subject of the discourse, and this fact, too, is established early. It is typical in American Sign Language to establish the important principals of an action or a narrative early. Sentences which leave the subject of the sentence or the topic under discussion in doubt until the sentence is half finished are not good Sign Language sentences. They may not be very good sentences in any language, but it is quite permissible in English to begin a sentence with several words that do nothing to clarify what is being discussed or even who the subject is. In English, for example, one might begin this paragraph, "Upon the invitation of a friend of mine named Harry, I flew last Wednesday from Washington, D.C., to Ohio." In American Sign Language it is inappropriate to delay the important information in such a manner. *Fly* is the same sign as the sign for *airplane*.

to O-H-I-O The preposition *to* touches the tip of the right index finger to the tip of the left index finger. *O-H-I-O* is likely to be localized somewhere off to the right, and the left index finger, which is already extended for the sign for *to,* may point to the right hand as it fingerspells *O-H-I-O.*

from Washington, D.C. *From* draws the curved right index finger back toward the body from the extended left index finger. *Washington, D.C.,* is signed by touching the right "W" to the right shoulder and then circling it in front of the right shoulder. The letters, *D* and *C* may be added.

What-for The sign for *for* touches the right fingertip to the forehead and then turns it down and forward in a small arc. Executed with a questioning expression, the sign means *what-for, why?* In the present text it was repeated twice for emphasis. By asking the question, *why?* or *what-for?* one can effectively avoid either a causal clause (I went to Ohio *because* someone invited me) or a purpose clause (I went to Ohio *in order* to make some videotapes).

Me man have friend man name H-A-R-R-Y *Me* is signed as indicated previously. The next sign, *man,* may be an intrusion. The material was generated extemporaneously, and some of the same kinds of false starts or incomplete sentences that one ordinarily finds in spoken English will, of course, also occur in Sign Language discourse. Later *man* is referenced and named as *H-A-R-R-Y,* which is fingerspelled. There is a possibility, however, that the reference to *man* at this point is deliberate. It has already been mentioned that American Sign Language usage prefers to name all

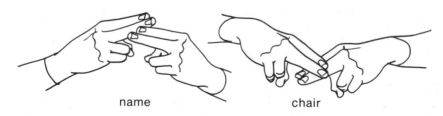

name   chair

FIG. 43. *The orientation of the hands sometimes serves as a distinctive feature, as can be seen in the pair of signs,* **name** *and* **chair.**

of the principals before going into much detail about them. It would be permissible for the sake of clarity to indicate at this point that the narrative concerns *me* and my flight to Ohio, but it also concerns the other *man,* Harry, who invited me to come to Ohio. *Have* is signed by touching the fingertips of both hands to the chest. *Name* crosses the fingers of the two "H" hands so as to form the shape of X. It has been said that this is the derivation of the sign. The sign for *name* when contrasted with the sign for *chair* illustrates that the orientation of the hands may constitute a distinctive feature in American Sign Language. *Chair* and *name* are signed with the same hand configurations with the same movement in the same location, but in *chair* the palms face downward while in *name* the palms face left and right (see Fig. 43).

He invite me By this time *Harry* has been localized off to the right so that pronominal references can be made by simply pointing in that direction. *Invite* is signed by moving the right hand, palm up, from the signer's body toward the position for *Harry.* Ordinarily *invite* is signed toward the signer's body, but this is one of several signs whose direction of movement can be altered so as to take into account who invited whom. In this case the signer is the object of the invitation, and the execution of the sign plainly indicates that. Nevertheless, *me* may be added after *invite* just to make sure that there is no misunderstanding.

for make T-V T-V movie *For* here is the same sign as *What-for* used previously. Here the sign clearly indicates purpose. The combination *for make* is comparable to the English infinitive construction, *to make,* which also indicates purpose. *T-V* has been taken over into American Sign Language as the "Sign" for *television.* It is tempting to drop the quotation marks and argue that such fingerspelling is signing, but the criteria for making such a decision are lacking. But there are enough instances of fingerspelling that do not seem to be simply a transliteration of English to make a case for a status for fingerspelling as an integral feature of the manual system of communication used by deaf persons. Here, for example, it is repeated, *T-V T-V.* Such repetition may take into account the brief duration of time required for spelling the two letters T and V, and in order to give the receiver an adequate opportunity to catch it, it is spelled twice. *Make* is signed by striking the right fist on top of the left fist as the two hands are twisted back and forth at the wrists. *Movie* has two different signs available in American Sign Language. One rubs the fingers of the two "5" hands back and forth in opposite directions so as to imitate the flickering effect of a motion picture. The other sign rests the heel of the right "5" hand on the back of the left fist and waves it back and forth briefly.

Me like O-K accept *Me* is signed as previously. *Like* may be an inaccurate translation of the Sign Language text. The signer placed his right palm against his chest briefly. Taken out of context, it would be construed as *my,* but that does not fit the present context. It is clearly tied to the subsequent sign for *accept,* which also brings the hand toward the signer's chest. The implication is clearly that this is a personal matter requiring some thought and a decision. The facial expression is contemplative. The *O-K* is another example of fingerspelling that appears to be very much like signing. *Accept* draws the fingertips of the right hand together as the hand is brought in contact with the chest.

All right This sign also means *right, morally right.* The right hand, palm facing left, is moved forward across the upturned left palm. For *all right* in the sense of *O-K,* the right hand may be turned upward in an arc as the sign is executed, and the facial expression may indicate a terminal juncture.

Me fly long *Me fly* is signed as indicated previously. *Long* strokes the right index finger up the left forearm toward the left shoulder. This sign is generally restricted to *long time.* Length in space is generally indicated by drawing the "L" hands apart so as to represent the length of whatever is being discussed.

three hour The numeral three is formed by the middle finger, index finger, and thumb of the right hand. The hand configuration may be held as a *three* as the sign for *hour* is executed. Ordinarily, hour is signed by tracing a circle with the right index finger on the left palm. The sign may be pluralized by showing a numeral, *two, three, four,* etc., either before or after signing *hour,* or the sign for *hour* may be executed with the right hand showing the numeral at the same time. Since the modifier, *three,* plainly marks *hour* as plural, no other plural marker is required.

fly fly fly fly The sign for *fly* is executed again in the narrative, this time with a slow, jerky movement going all the way across the front of the signer's face. The manner in which the sign is executed conveys the desired impression that it was a long and tedious flight.

Me tired *Me* is signed as before. *Tired* touches the fingertips of both hands to the rib cage on either side of the chest and then rolls the hands forward as if the fingers are too weak to support the weight of the hands.

Sit, read book The sign for *sit* is the same as the sign for *chair.* A variation of the sign has the right "H" hand's fingers bent over as they rest on the back of the fingers of the left "H" hand, perhaps to indicate the legs dangling over the edge of the chair. *Read* moves the fingertips of the right "V" hand across the left palm as if scanning a page. The movement may go from left to right and from line to line as if following lines of type in a printed text. *Book* is motivated by the covers: both hands are held together, palms facing, and they are opened as a book is opened.

Read me bored *Read* is repeated a second time. *Me* is signed as before. *Bored* twists the right index finger against the bridge of the nose. The little finger may be extended for emphasis.

Anyway The right hand slaps the fingers of the left hand back and forth several times. The sign is used here as a signal that the narrator is about to move on to a new topic. The same sign also means *indifferent* or *it makes no difference.*

Me arrive here O-H-I-O *Arrive* holds the left hand, palm up, in front of the body, and the back of the right hand is dropped down into it. *Here* circles both hands, palms up, in front of the body close to the body. Executing this sign just a little closer to the body than is typical for signs executed in front of the body is helpful for making the sign completely unambiguous. *O-H-I-O* is fingerspelled.

He H-A-R-R-Y Harry is still localized to the right of the signer, but it has been some time since a reference has been made to him. Therefore, after pointing to that location again, his name is spelled again.

He have truck The pointing signal is used again for the pronominal reference. *Have* is signed as before. *Truck* is not easy to sign unambiguously. Pupils at Kendall School for the Deaf in Washington, D.C., hold the steering wheel more horizontally, as is typical in a truck. They may also puff out their cheeks to indicate the size of the vehicle they imagine that they are steering.

big truck In the present text, in addition to body cues that the vehicle was larger than a car, the adjective *big* is added. The two "L" hands are drawn apart from each other with a flourish.

We-two drive his home *We-two* is a commonly used sign in American Sign Language. The right hand is held with the index and middle fingers extended, palm up. It is moved back and forth in a horizontal plane, the index finger referencing the other person and the middle finger referencing the body of the signer. It is a dual, for which English has no grammatical equivalent. *Drive* is signed the same as *truck. His* uses the open palm as the possessive marker. It is directed to the right, where Harry has been localized. *Home* touches the fingertips of the right "AND" hand to the lips and to the cheek.

Truly nice *Truly* brings the vertical right index finger forward from the lips. It might also be translated *very* or *really. Nice* is signed by stroking the right palm across the upturned left palm away from the body. The same sign also means *clean*. *Nice* is often signed slowly, as if to emphasize the feel of the hands across one another as the sign is executed.

big The two "L" hands are drawn apart from each other. To emphasize the sign, the motion is made non-symmetrical, with the one hand leading the other in the separation.

We-two arrive sit talk *We-two, arrive,* and *sit* are signed as before. *Talk* is signed by moving the vertical fingers of the right "4" hand, palm left, forward from the mouth several times.

drink converse *Drink* is ordinarily signed by tipping the "C" hand to the lips. When an alcoholic beverage is implied, the crooked thumb and index finger may be tipped to the mouth, probably reflecting the typical shape of a cocktail glass. The Sign Language sentence, *You want drink?* with *drink* signed with the thumb and index finger tipped to the mouth may be construed as an invitation to have an alcoholic beverage. *Converse* uses both hands, palms up, moved toward each other in front of the body several times in a casual manner. This sign is used primarily to indicate a casual conversation, not a serious discussion. A *conversation* in a more formal sense may move the upright index fingers back and forth alternately in front of the mouth.

Enjoy The palms of both hands are rubbed over the chest and stomach.

True night *True* is the same as *truly*. *Night* tucks the right arm under the left forearm, indicating that the sun is going below the horizon. The lateness of the hour can be indicated by the length of the movement of the right arm.

time one Clock time is ordinarily indicated by first signing *time* and then indicating by means of a numeral what time it is. This eliminates any ambiguity, since *one time* may mean something entirely different. *Time* is signed by touching the right index finger to the place on the left wrist where a watch is likely to be worn. *One* holds the right index finger upright.

night The sign for *night* is repeated again for emphasis.

Me afraid *Afraid* is signed by thrusting both "5" hands, palms facing the body, toward each other so that they cross in front of the body, shielding it.

morning oversleep *Morning* brings the right forearm up from under the left arm, indicating the rising sun. *Oversleep* brings the right "F" hand up from under the left arm in a movement similar to *morning*, but the right hand continues upward to a higher level, and the left arm as a reference point drops out in the final position of the sign. The execution of the sign conveys the impression that the sun is already up in the sky before one knew about it.

Me afraid The statement *me afraid* is repeated again for emphasis. Such repetition is not necessary in Sign Language, but it does occur frequently.

Me get-up time seven *Get-up* is signed here with tensed muscles, especially at the beginning of the execution of the sign. This slow beginning with evident expenditure of energy conveys the notion that this is a customary or habitual activity on the part of the signer. It could be translated, "I habitually get up at seven o'clock." The use of muscle tone to alter the meaning of a sign is a strategy of American Sign Language usage that is often missed by persons who are not native speakers. As a strategy for expressing one's self effectively in Sign Language it is typically not acquired until after a great deal of practice and familiarity with Sign Language usage. *Time seven* follows the same sequence as *time one*.

Me bathe finish shave finish *Bathe* is motivated by the act of bathing: both fists rub up and down on the chest. *Shave* uses the right hand to represent a razor and the motions of shaving are imitated. *Finish* turns both "5" hands over with a flick of the wrist. It is commonly used in American Sign Language to represent an action completed in the past. It can also mean *done*.

We-two drive for T-V T-V place building *We-two drive* is signed as indicated previously. *For* is used here to indicate the destination. This is a variation on the general meaning of purpose. It is signed as before. *T-V* is repeated twice again. *Place* is signed by tracing an area in front of the body with a symmetrical movement of both "P" hands or with the thumbs of both "A" hands. *Building* is signed by placing the fingers of each hand alternately on top of the fingers of the other hand as they are raised upward in front of the body. It has been said that the sign is derived from the act of laying brick. The fingertips of the "H" hands may be used.

True nice These are signed as before.

But me machinery much *But* crosses the index fingers and then pulls them apart. The reference to *me* may have been an anticipation of the forthcoming subject. *Machinery* meshes the curved "5" hands together in front of the body in a rocking motion that may represent cog wheels meshing their teeth. *Much* is signed here in a variant on the usual execution. Usually *much* is signed by moving the two hands, palms facing, apart from each other in front of the body. This is typically used for *much* in the sense of a large *amount*. But in this case the machinery is spread out all over the studio. It is not something that can be indicated as a large amount between the two hands. Therefore, the sign inverts the hands so that the palms are down, and the two hands move forward at angles from the body as if taking in a great quantity of space.

me not-yet see before *Not-yet* is generally signed with one hand. The palm is facing backward, and the fingers point downward, and the hand is moved backward at the waist several times. The association with the temporal marker represented by the side of the body is clear. Something that has not yet happened is clearly in the past. For emphasis, the sign may be executed with both hands moved backward at the sides of the body. *See* is executed by pointing the fingertips of the right "V" hand to the eyes and then moving the hand forward from the face. *Before* uses the left hand as a point of reference and draws the right hand toward the body from the

left. As an alternative, the right hand may be moved back over the right shoulder.

Me surprise The conventional sign for *surprise* touches the index finger of each hand to the thumb, places the hands next to the eyes, and then draws them apart as if to represent the widening eyes that may accompany a *surprise*. As an alternative "0" hands may be placed next to the eyes and opened into "C" hands.

Have one two three four list for C-A-M-E-R-A *Have* is signed as indicated previously. *One, two, three, four* are counted off one by one for emphasis. Then *list* is signed: the horizontal fingers of both "4" hands are drawn apart from one another vertically, with the right hand moving downward from the left. *For* again indicates purpose, but this time the purpose of the equipment is implicit in the name for the equipment, namely that they are *cameras*. *C-A-M-E-R-A* is fingerspelled.

Have many many *Many* is signed by starting with a clenched fist in one or both hands and then throwing the fingers upward into "5" configurations one or more times. Here it is suggested that the sign be repeated at least twice.

T-V T-V movie Again, *T-V* is repeated twice. *Movie* is signed in either of the ways indicated previously. This represents a change of subject matter again. Such changes in topic of conversation are often signaled by a change in facial expression, shifting the body position, hunching the shoulders, or nodding.

Me try fingerspell big-word *Try* is signed by bringing both fists forward laboriously in front of the body. This is another instance of a sign in which the muscle tone adds measurably to the meaning. *Fingerspell* holds the right "5" hand, palm down, in front of the shoulder, and the fingers are wiggled. The hand may be moved sideways left and right a short distance one or more times to indicate the spelling of different words. *Big-word* is a colloquial expression. The right "Y" hand is placed against the left index finger. The right "Y" hand is also used for the sign for *measure,* and the left index finger is used for the ordinary sign for *word*. The combination of the two leaves the impression of a word that has been measured and found to be too big.

Me dummy fingerspell me *Dummy* here is signed by sticking the thumb of the right "5" hand in the opening of the left "0" hand and throwing the fingers of the right "5" hand back toward the body with a twist of the wrist. This sign may be socially restricted. The same sign executed at the right ear is used as a derogative term for *deaf,* although it is sometimes used by deaf people themselves in jest. The *fingerspell me* helps to make certain that the self-deprecating comment applies to the fingerspelling of big words.

Movie finish The signs for these terms are the same as described previously. Again the sign *finish* is used for an action completed in the past. In English, this would be a past perfect tense, "When the filming had been completed."

Me want see school around area *Me* is signed as before. *Want* draws the curved "5" hands, palms up, toward the body. *See* is signed as described previously. *School* is signed by clapping the hands together. *Around area* are natural gestures designed to designate an area in front of the signer's body that represents the area that is referenced. The facial expression, eye movement, and body orientation all play a role in referencing the area in question.

Me visit look *Visit* is signed by circling the "V" hands alternately in circles outward from the body. *Look* is signed by turning the right "V" hand so that the fingertips

point outward, and directing the "gaze" of the right "V" hand in various directions. In effect, the two fingers represent the eyes, and the direction in which they are pointed indicates the direction in which the signer is saying that he is looking.

Me hope later *Hope* is ordinarily signed as a compound, derived from *think* and *wait.* The right index finger is touched to the forehead, and then the two hands, palms facing, are waved toward each other by bending at the knuckles. In the present case, a colloquial expression, more a natural gesture than a sign, is used to signify *hope:* Both hands cross index and middle fingers in the manner of "keeping one's fingers crossed." *Later* makes a forward movement, a time marker, with the index finger of the right hand, as the thumb makes imaginary contact with the left palm. This sign is usually executed with the right thumb in contact with the left palm, but this is not necessary. A twist of the wrist with the index finger rocking forward will be construed as meaning *after while, later* regardless of the position of the right hand in relation to the left.

will fly The future marker is invoked here to indicate the hope-for event. The right hand, palm left, is moved forward from the body. *Fly* is signed as indicated previously.

again O-H-I-O For *again* the left hand is held, palm up, and the right hand is brought up in an arc and then down into the left palm so that the fingertips of the right hand strike the middle of the left palm. *O-H-I-O* is fingerspelled.

VOCABULARY

1. accept (HH-218, TO-331)
2. afraid (HH-48, TO-177)
3. again (HH-3ɔ2, TO-191)
4. ago (HH-118, TO-205)
5. airplane (HH-1, TO-651)
6. all right (HH-302, TO-60)
7. anyway (HH-169, TO-196)
8. area (see text)
9. around (see text)
10. arrive (HH-221, TO-365)
11. bathe (HH-99, TO-117)
12. because (HH-318, TO-13)
13. before (HH-30, TO-204)
14. big (HH-473, TO-429)
15. big word (see text)
16. book (HH-237, TO-181)
17. bored (HH-102)
18. building (HH-159, TO-352)
19. camera (fingerspell)
20. chair (HH-206, TO-624)
21. clean (HH-112, TO-48)
22. converse (see text)
23. drink (see text)
24. drive (HH-375, TO-160)
25. dummy (see text)
26. enjoy (HH-42, TO-255)
27. fingerspell (HH-418, TO-148)
28. finish (HH-214, TO-174)
29. fly (HH-1, TO-651)
30. for (HH-404, TO-18)
31. four (TO-p. 4)
32. friend (HH-314, TO-638)
33. from (HH-16, TO-33)
34. get up (see text)
35. Harry (fingerspell)
36. have (HH-292, TO-268)
37. he (HH-403)
38. here (HH-142, TO-58)
39. his (HH-469)
40. home (HH-489, TO-241)
41. hope (HH-12, TO-454)
42. hour (HH-422, TO-533)
43. in order to (HH-404, TO-18)
44. indifferent (HH-169, TO-196)
45. invite (HH-261, TO-355)
46. it makes no difference (HH-169, TO-196)
47. later (HH-262, TO-531)
48. like (HH-80, TO-394)
49. list (see text)
50. long (see text)
51. look (HH-4]3, TO-209)
52. machinery (HH-105, TO-248)
53. make (HH-210, TO-298)
54. man (HH-238, TO-145)
55. many (HH-34, TO-657)
56. me (HH-192, TO-2)
57. morally right (HH-302, TO-60)
58. movie (HH-61, TO-587)
59. much (HH-473, TO-167)
60. name (HH-385, TO-621)
61. nice (HH-112, TO-48)
62. night (HH-308, TO-186)
63. not yet (HH-166, TO-360)
64. Ohio (fingerspell)
65. OK (fingerspell)
66. one (TO-p. 4)
67. oversleep (see text)
68. place (HH-44, TO-433)
69. read (HH-208, TO-585)
70. really (HH-291, TO-219)
71. right (HH-302, TO-60)
72. school (HH-277, TO-49)
73. see (HH-381, TO-207)
74. seven (TO- p. 4)
75. shave (TO-643)
76. sit (HH-206, TO-624)
77. surprise (HH-207, TO-664)
78. talk (see text)
79. television (see text)
80. three (TO-p. 4)
81. time (HH-187, TO-595)
82. tired (HH-63, TO-278)
83. to (HH-240, TO-30)
84. truck (see text)
85. truly (HH-291, TO-219)
86. try (HH-149, TO-154)
87. TV (fingerspell)
88. two (TO-p. 4)
89. visit (HH-227, TO-300)

90. want (HH-448, TO-173)
91. Washington, D.C. (TO-443)
92. we two (see text)
93. Wednesday (HH-328, TO-267)
94. what for (HH-404, TO-18)
95. why (HH-8, TO-16)

EXERCISES

Sign the following sentences and provide an English translation.

1. Makes-no-difference time me get-up bathe shave.

2. What-for what-for H-A-R-R-Y surprise? We-two oversleep.

3. Three time drive truck visit Washington, D.C.

4. See T-V, T-V movie, enjoy much; man make machine for airplane, true airplane. Me surprise.

5. We-two drive Washington, D.C. What-for drive, What-for drive. Me want fly.

6. Man he not-yet tired. He fly fly not-yet two hours. Not-yet tired.

7. Man he invite friend seven for have drink; drink finish, drive around area; see T-V movie place.

8. Me finish school, me go home tired; want nice chair; read book.

9. Man long time friend, long time friend; converse two night ago; converse, converse, converse; enjoy.

10. Building big; have place for machinery much; have place for C-A-M-E-R-A many; building big T-V building.

RECOMMENDED READINGS ────────────

Furth, H. G. *Deafness and learning: A psychosocial approach.* Belmont, Calif.: Wadsworth, 1973.

Furth, H. G. *Thinking without language: Psychological implications of deafness.* New York: Free Press, 1966.

Hoemann, H. W., & Hoemann, S. A. *Sign Language Flash Cards.* Silver Spring, Md.: National Association of the Deaf, 1973.

Klima, E. S., & Bellugi, U. The signs of language in child and chimpanzee. In T. Alloway, L. Krames, & P. Pliner (Eds.), *Communication and affect: A comparative approach.* New York: Academic Press, 1972, 67-96.

Mallery, G. Sign Language among North American Indians. In J. W. Powell (Ed.), *First Annual Report of the Bureau of American Ethnology.* Washington, D.C.: The Smithsonian Institution, 1881, 263-552.

O'Rourke, T. J. (Ed.), *Psycholinquistics and total communication: The state of the art.* Washington, D.C.: American Annals of the Deaf, 1972.

O'Rourke, T. J. *A basic course in manual communication.* Revised Edition. Silver Spring, Md.: National Association of the Deaf, 1973.

Schlesinger, H. S., & Meadow, K. P. *Sound and sign: Childhood deafness and mental health.* Berkeley, Calif.: University of California Press, 1972.

Stokoe, W. C. *Semiotics and human Sign Languages.* The Hague: Mouton, 1972.

Stokoe, W. C. *Sign Language structure: An outline of the visual communication systems of the American deaf. Studies in Linquistics, Occasional Papers: No. 8.* Buffalo, N.Y.: University of Buffalo Press, 1960.

Stokoe, W. C., Casterline, D., & Croneberg, C. *A dictionary of American Sign Language on linquistic principles.* Washington, D.C.: Gallaudet College Press, 1965.

Index

mental activity, 2, 40, 59
Methodical Sign Language, 55, 104
modulation, 20, 22, 28, 41, 76, 97
motivation of signs, 5, 54, 103
movement denoting a verb, 67
muscle tension and muscle tone, 41, 106, 115
name signs, 52, 90
narrative order, 43, 69
National Association of the Deaf, x, 11, 56
natural gesture, 8, 10, 15, 23, 46, 67, 68, 69, 85, 117
negation by shaking the head, 38
negation by turning the palms away, 33
noun-adjective sequence, 6, 29, 68, 104
numerals, 15, 20, 32, 33, 38, 46, 70, 94
one-handed signing, 83
order constraints, 33, 66
ordinal adverbs, 70
ordinal numerals, 15, 20, 33, 94
origin of signs, 103
O'Rourke, Terrence J., 11, 120
pantomime, 69, 78, 85
paralanguage, 56
parts of speech, 102
past action continuing to the present, 91
past marker, 2, 18, 21, 28, 30, 38, 66, 76, 90, 97, 102
paternalism, 98
pause, 4, 7, 29, 32, 64, 81
peddling, 43, 70
person marker, 7, 21, 64, 82
pinched lips, 33, 43, 44
pluralization by adding a numeral, 32, 66, 68, 97, 114
pluralization by adding an adjective, 52, 56, 58
pluralization by adding the sign, *group*, 18
pluralization by making a horizontal movement, 7, 54, 84
pluralization by pointing, 39
pluralization by repetition, 7, 38, 40, 45, 57, 84
pluralization inferred from the context, 77
positioning, 65
possessive marker, 7, 14, 18, 34, 40, 82, 90, 92, 104
prepositions, 3, 28, 64, 78, 84
present progressive, 4
present time marker, 14
pronominal reference, 14, 92, 112, 114
puffed cheeks, 44, 114

purpose, 7, 91, 112
quotation marks, 98
raised eyebrows, 43, 65
rapport, 16, 19, 30, 54, 64, 81, 91
reflexive, 80, 103
Registry of Interpreters for the Deaf, 104
regional variation in signs, 15, 40, 91
repetition compensating for lost movement, 46, 76
repetition for changed meaning, 5, 22, 31, 44, 52, 64, 71
repetition for clarity, 113
repetition for continuing action, 5, 41, 69, 107, 114
repetition for emphasis, 41, 115
repetition for pluralization, 7, 38, 40, 45, 57, 84
reverse interpreting, 104
rhythm, 8, 67
role playing, 31, 32, 105, 107
Schlesinger, Hilde S., 120
seasons of the year, 15, 53
sentence structure in Sign Language, 43, 47, 65, 72
serial order, 67
Seventh World Congress, 20
Sign Language Flash Cards, x, 11
Signed English, 33, 58
sign order, 33, 66
signs denoting feeling or emotion, 40, 45, 59
signs denoting mental activity, 2, 40, 59
simultaneous execution of signs, 92, 105
socially restricted signs, 6, 9, 45, 117
spatial domain, 76, 92
spatial organization, 9, 40, 43, 47
spatial relations, 3, 47, 105
speech with signing, 97
squinting to modify the meaning, 112
Stokoe, William C., Jr., 2, 57, 120
structural elements of signs, 2, 57
subordination, 42
superlative, 53
temporal frame of reference, 18, 30, 76, 90, 92, 93, 95, 112
temporal marker, 22, 45, 91
temporal relations, 105
terminal juncture, 113
time lines, 2, 30, 31, 90, 105
translating, 104
transparency of meaning of signs, 54
World Deaf Federation, 56